Dilemmas of Life

Deciding what's right and what's wrong

Dilemmas of Life

Deciding what's right and what's wrong

David Cook

Inter-Varsity Press

INTER-VARSITY PRESS
38 De Montfort Street, Leicester LE1 7GP, England

Scripture quotations in this publication are from the Holy Bible, New International Version. Copyright © 1973, 1978, 1984 International Bible Society. Published by Hodder & Stoughton Ltd.

First published 1990
Reprinted 1991, 1997

British Library Cataloguing in Publication Data
Cook, E. David (Edward David), *1947–*
    Dilemmas of Life: deciding what's right and what's wrong
    1. Christian ethics
    I. Title
    241

ISBN 0-85110-838-5

Set in Linotype Ehrhardt

Typeset in Great Britain by Parker Typesetting Service, Leicester

Printed in Great Britain by Cox & Wyman Ltd, Reading, Berkshire

Inter-Varsity Press is the book-publishing division of the Universities and Colleges Christian Fellowship (formerly the Inter-Varsity Fellowship), a student movement linking Christian Unions in universities and colleges throughout the United Kingdom and the Republic of Ireland, and a member movement of the International Fellowship of Evangelical Students. For information about local and national activities write to UCCF, 38 De Montfort Street, Leicester LE1 7GP.

Contents

To my sister Linda
and her family

Preface

When books get written, a number of people are involved. It is important that they are recorded and thanked. Inter-Varsity Press enthusiastically encouraged the project. The Christian Colleges Consortium, especially Carl Lundquist, gave me the opportunity to test out the material in thirteen colleges in the United States. Maggie Wright did some of the typing. My family put up, as always, with the early mornings and late nights. I dedicate this book to my sister, Linda, and her family. She no longer has to do my typing, but she and her husband cope well with trying to discern right and wrong in a changing world.

David Cook

Introduction
Morality matters

*I*f we open a newspaper, turn on the radio or television, or begin a discussion in our homes, pubs or work, then it won't be very long until morality rears its head. What is right or wrong, good or bad, matters deeply to us and we are all too ready to express our views even when we are not asked. A typical news broadcast may bring us information about continuing drought in Ethiopia, a military coup attempt in the Philippines, the latest release from a psychiatric unit of a refusenik from the Ukraine, strikes in the Yorkshire coal mines, and infidelities of a presidential candidate in the United States. All of these call for and evoke some kind of moral response.

At the national level, when we examine a nation's legislative programme, we find that moral questions soon arise. Whether the National Health Service is under-funded, what rights children have to be safeguarded from child abuse, whether or not to reduce the limit allowing abortions to eighteen weeks, and what kind of trading should be permitted on a Sunday are all issues which have a moral dimension and affect our moral sensitivities.

Indeed, if we reflect on the changes in law made by Parliament over homosexual behaviour, divorce and abortion, we can begin to see the impact on moral attitudes and behaviour which a government can have. A government can set the tone morally. By refusing to reintroduce capital punishment, Parliament in Britain is trying to uphold a view of right and wrong which is not shared by the majority of the country. Parliament argues that it would be less civilized and a step back morally to reinstitute capital punishment.

The other side of that is the way in which law and changes in law express the changes in moral outlook of the people of a nation. Law can be the expression of where a society is morally. We frame laws because society as a whole feels that those issues need to be dealt with. The debate over legislation for experiments on embryos and fetuses is a response from scientists and the public expressing concern over what is happening and could happen. The need for moral guidelines expressed in law led to the Warnock Report and the promise of some kind of legislation. The fact that it has taken so long to get to the law-making stage shows how hard it is to know what public opinion is and will accept. But any laws will reflect something of the moral views of the community. Law and morality do have a close inter-relationship, and inter-react with each other.

The churches at the local and national level also reflect the importance of ethical issues and of responding to them. Each of the main denominations has some kind of Board for Social Responsibility. In the synods, assemblies, convocations, councils and conferences of the churches the last twenty years have seen major concentration on matters of morality and much less discussion of the previously all-pervasive theme of liturgical change and renewal. The church papers, denominational reports and the teaching from pulpits and in house groups reflect a keen focus on morality and how to apply Christian thinking and belief in the complexity of the modern world. Christianity is about how to live and what we ought to do.

At the personal and individual level it is no different. Every family unit knows or is directly affected by people whose marriage has broken down and those who live in a whole variety of relationships. Many of us will face major job changes and even unemployment and redundancy. We may be affected by economic retrenchment and the impact on health and welfare services. But, perhaps most of all, we can hardly fail to be confronted with major moral issues about justice, human rights, sexuality, life and death, work and unemployment, economic systems and relationships and a whole host of individual, community, national and international ethical issues and questions. Morality matters.

The problem is that when the problems seem *greater* in number, urgency and complexity, we seem *less able* to reflect on and resolve them. Our moral apparatus and thinking seem to be woefully inadequate for the task we require them to perform. Yet we all make moral decisions and pass moral judgments all the time. This may be no grandiose affair. It may be nothing more than telling each other what we think and feel about what we read in the papers and see on the television. But on what do we base our moral judgments? What are the things that we rely on as we try to think through ethical decisions? What is our morality and where does it come from?

This book is an attempt to examine some of the main features of morality. It is a kind of map of what we use as we face moral questions. It is a critical map, for it tries to see the positive and the negative sides in each area. The strengths and weaknesses of different approaches are weighed and recorded. But this is not a book on moral philosophy which is not rooted in life as we know and live it. It is grounded in what we are doing and the ways in which we face up to our modern world. In the end, it is not just a description, even if that description is present and given a critical form. There is a prescription, but that only emerges in the light of the analysis. The way to test the adequacy of the book is to ask whether the description in each chapter is fair, whether the criticisms are justified, and whether the prescription will make a difference or not.

Chapter *one*

Right *and wrong in principle*

*I*f newspapers are anything to go by the main issues that matter to most of us are questions of right and wrong. Morality matters, whether it is the latest scandal about politicians or the need for another Band Aid to help the starving in Africa. It's the same with television, for it deals with the moral problems facing us. *EastEnders* and *Dallas* in very different ways purport to tell us of the dilemmas facing people and how they are to decide what to do. Right and wrong are not a matter of thinking about things. They matter so much because they concern what we are to do. How we are to live and respond to the world around us is crucial.

Morality is about the relationships between people. It is the fact that we relate to each other, and that this raises questions about what is proper and improper in our relationships, that makes right and wrong so important. To treat other people properly is part of what right behaviour means. When relationships break down and go wrong, then bad behaviour and failures in morality lie not far away.

At the end of 1988 a bomb blasted a Pan-Am jumbo jet from the sky over the small Scottish town of Lockerbie. The bomb was almost certainly planted by a terrorist group. Is it right to kill people for the sake of a political cause? Is it not wrong to kill innocent people who have no part in the issue at stake? The way the passengers were treated by the bombers and their accomplices was surely wrong. But what of the innocent folks of Lockerbie preparing for Christmas before they were so cruelly killed by plane wreckage? Terrorist actions affect many people who are not intended victims or targets. But the bad behaviour did not stop with the terrorists. The roads round Lockerbie were blocked, and vital rescue services were hampered from reaching the scenes of the disaster, because sightseers flocked to see the tragedy. Then we heard of men being arrested for stealing parts of the wreckage necessary for the forensic scientists in their grisly work of knowing when, where and how the bomb exploded. Some even stole the belongings of those killed in the crash. Our natural horror at all of these actions shows that we do have very clear ideas of right and wrong about how we treat and relate to each other. Even the dead are entitled to proper respect and treatment. Morality and our behaviour towards each other are inextricably linked.

Naturally this realm of how we treat each other expands into wider realms of how we treat our world, our environment and the other beings who share our habitat. Human relationships with animals and the natural order of things raise moral issues of right and wrong. Should animals be killed for furs? The loss of many species is directly related to hunters and the supply of the fashion trade. Should we use animals for food? Are the conditions we keep such animals in important? Battery hens, force-fed geese, hormonally treated cattle, are all at the mercy of the ever-increasing human demands for more and better.

But it is not just the animal world which is affected by human behaviour. The rivers, the air, the land itself are all polluted by the waste we create from our industrial and leisure activities. The cars we drive, the deodorants we use, and the rubbish we throw away all affect our environment. We rape the earth of its precious resources and then pollute the world with what is left. How we treat our world and all that is in it matters to us, and our behaviour is significant and important.

Part of this significance and importance lies in the fact that morality matters to us in our relationships because it deals with what we *feel* about things. We feel concerned about things that are important to us. Things that relate to our relationships with other people are matters of how we feel and what we feel about other people. There is a close relationship between what we feel and how we view right and wrong. What is good and bad as far as we are concerned is related to what we feel positively and negatively about. Politicians, political parties and pressure groups know how strongly what we feel motivates us. There are themes that 'move' audiences and create support. It may be 'law and order' at the Conservative Party Conference, trade union rights at a Labour Party Conference, or ecological issues in the Green Party. It was no accident that in the marvellous Band Aid concerts the music was interspersed with powerful, emotive pictures of starvation, death and dying. Bob Geldof knew that when people felt the wrong, they would give generously. So they did.

But feelings are not all that are involved in morality. To make a proper moral decision involves knowing certain facts about that situation. What is the case and what is actually happening and likely to occur matter in making the moral decisions we face. If I push my friend to the ground during a country walk and he ends up in the mud, his face splattered and his clothes ruined, it is unlikely he will feel thrilled by what has been done to him. But if he then discovers that he was in the direct line of fire of some pheasant shooters and my prompt action had, in fact, saved his life, then the new information would put a totally different complexion on things and radically affect what he felt about what had happened. Thus morality is about facts as well as about feelings.

It seems, then, that morality is about things that matter, about our relationships, and about what we feel and how we understand what is going on around us. It would seem that morality is no great problem if this is all that there is to worry about. If I understand the exact situation, and feel correctly in the light of that, and am concerned to make sure I get the right answers in my relationships with other people, then I should arrive at the correct conclusions. The problem is what we mean by the 'correct' solution.

This last paragraph makes it seem as if morality is an easy affair. We simply look at the moral dilemma and then make up our mind and we arrive at the right answer. Would that it were so! The feminist argues that to have an abortion is every woman's fundamental right. A woman is free to do whatever she wishes with her own body. A Roman Catholic doctor suggests that abortion is an issue not so much of the rights of women, but of the slaughter of the innocent. To induce an abortion is seen as committing murder, and nothing can justify the taking of innocent life, least of all the demand for rights.

Some people believe that it is totally and utterly immoral to have nuclear weapons and to threaten to use them in any circumstances. For them, the only morally correct behaviour is to abandon nuclear weapons once and for all. There are equally many who feel just as strongly that such abandonment is immoral foolishness. For them, we have a moral responsibility to defend our nation, homes and families. We are faced with a nuclear threat from those who would seek to destroy and undermine our freedom and way of life. Thus we must use whatever weapons we can in order to maintain peace and justice. For such people, nuclear deterrence is fundamental to a proper defence of our way of life and the values we have fought to preserve. It would be immoral to throw away our only means of the threat and the reality of retaliation. Only such a threat and its reality can deter and so ensure peace.

What is evident from these two examples is that morality is not a clear-cut case of all believing the one thing and arriving at the same answers to the problems that face us. The problem is that it often seems as if there are as many different answers to moral questions as there are people who face these problems. Different people come to different solutions to exactly the same kind of dilemmas. But if that is the case, how are we to live with each other?

The rest of this book is an attempt to look at the ways in which we decide about right and wrong in our world today. It would be tempting to imagine that there was some golden time in the past when making moral decisions was easy and straightforward. Even if that were true, it would not be of much help to us today. We face a complicated world where the dilemmas themselves are extremely difficult and where people come to so many different and contradictory answers to the questions they face. We shall try to chart the different kinds of answers that people give and how they arrive at those answers. It is the means of arriving at moral conclusions which matters here. We are trying to find out *why* people give different answers to questions about what is right and wrong, and *how* they decide what is good and bad.

We shall look at the conflict between principles and consequences as the basis for morality. We shall try to see how pleasure and happiness play a key role in moral decision-making. The particular challenges to morality from relativism and reductionism will be weighed and examined. Then the role of the individual will be explored.

My response to reading this list is to shout for help. The words don't mean very much and they seem to be a million miles away from the nitty gritty of decision-making. If that is your response too, please give the book a chance. There are simple and straight-forward ways of explaining what all these mean and how they actually affect us. If morality matters then it is important to read on and try to understand what is happening to us all. But if we only did that and arrived at a description of the situation we all face, then we would be little better off than we are now. We would know what was happening to us, but might not be able to do anything about it. It is important that we explore whether there is any way out of the morass of morality and any hope of a solid and adequate basis of morality. To try to respond to this concern we shall look at the ways in which Christians make moral decisions and what we can all learn from them. Perhaps then we shall find a reliable way of arriving at what is right and wrong.

Right is right and wrong is wrong

Children are great ones for asking questions. At first it is a delight that young people are so concerned to know what is going on and why. But as time goes by, it can become less than a delight. In fact, it is a pain. This is illustrated by the tale of the mother who took her child to the zoo for the day. The little boy was introduced to the rhinoceros and asked why they were called rhinoceros. The mother replied that she did not know. They went on to the elephants and again the child asked why they were called elephants. The mother again said that she did not know. Then they reached the hippopotamus and the inevitable question came and received the same answer. The little boy asked plaintively if his mother minded him asking all these questions The mother smiled indulgently and said she did not mind at all. After all, how else was he going to learn anything?

Listening to parents responding to children, one is struck by the way in which they start off. It all seems so sweetly reasonable at the start. They give pleasant answers to the child's questions and explain as best they can. The children, however, are not always easily satisfied and keep on asking things. Why? Why? Why? Eventually the parents' patience wears thin and they explode. 'Because I say so.' This is the end of the argument as far as the parents are concerned. It may not seem quite so satisfactory to the children.

The plea that we are to accept things just because we are told to do so is matched by a similar plea that we are to accept things because that is the way things are. This is the heart of the approach to morality which rests its basis on 'what is right is right because it is right and what is wrong is wrong because it is wrong'. There is and can be no further argument when we reach this point. Morality is supposed to be obvious.

Morality based on principles

If we return to the feminist and the Roman Catholic doctor and any discussion they might have on the issue of abortion, we can imagine the scenario. The feminist says that it is obvious that abortion is perfectly all right if the woman chooses it. After all, her argument goes, a woman has the right to do whatever she wants with her own body. The doctor might intervene and ask *why* it is the case that a woman has the right to do whatever she wants with her own body. The reply would come back, 'Because a woman has the right to do whatever she wants with her own body.' As far as the feminist is concerned, here is an absolute principle. It is obvious and right because it is right.

The doctor is working with another principle. He believes that life is sacred and to be preserved at all costs. For the doctor, abortion is murder and the taking of innocent life is wrong. The doctor will then inevitably reach the position that it is obvious that the taking of innocent life in an abortion is wrong. It is wrong because it is wrong.

There is an approach to morality which believes that we are dealing with absolute standards of right and wrong and goodness and badness. Morality is about knowing what these standards are and discerning the principles of right and wrong.

The great advantage of this approach is that, if it were true, it would make morality a straightforward affair. To settle a moral dispute all we would need to do would be to establish which principles were at stake, and, once we had seen clearly what the issues were, we would be able to reach agreement about what it was right to do.

This approach to morality is called the *deontological* approach. It states that there are certain things which we ought to do because they are right in themselves. There are equally certain things that we ought not to do because they are wrong in themselves. This idea that actions are right or wrong in themselves really means that there comes a point where it is obvious whether something is right or wrong. At that point there is no further need for, or even possibility of, argument or evidence. Literally, there is nothing more to be said. There is nothing more that needs to be said, for all that is necessary has been done and said. We should have reached the position in which we are able to see what is right and wrong for ourselves.

The sources of principles

There are many claimed sources for moral principles. They may come from authorities we recognize and allow to rule over us. They may come from an appeal to what is natural or usual. They may arise from what our consciences tell us.

The business of making moral decisions is a difficult one. We often feel that we don't really know what to think or how to go about it. There is therefore a sense of relief which can come if we can find an authority. This means that we allow someone else to tell us what to do rather than having to work everything out for ourselves. Students can do this with text-books. They can try to find the one book which gives the answer to the essay question they are supposed to be exploring. It makes life much easier if we have only one source for what we are to do and how we are to live.

When we are children we accept the authority of parents and those elder relatives we live beside. Their word is law and we do what they tell us without very much question. Then we go off to school and substitute teachers for parents. Everything and anything our teachers say is believed as gospel and we are willing to do whatever they tell us. Inevitably there comes a point where the parents and the teachers disagree about something and the child is faced with a dilemma. Which authority is to be accepted and believed? Authority is not uniform and does not always say the same thing.

Religious people look to their particular religion as the guide for their way of life. It may be the holy book, the holy person or founder, or the religious leadership and structures which provide the authority. In a way, the religious person is not trying to arrive at his or her own conclusions about morality unless these are firmly rooted and grounded in their particular religious tradition. For the Christian, moral authority is found in God. Morality is God's gift to us. What is right and wrong, good and bad are defined and delineated by reference to God. This means that at the heart of the Christian approach to morality lies revelation.

God reveals his moral standards to us. Christians then accept the authority of God's revelation. They believe that God's authority is trustworthy, reliable and to be accepted and obeyed.

God's moral revelation has many different forms. God reveals himself and his laws in the nature of the world, in human nature, in his dealings with his people, in the pages of Scripture and, most of all, in and through his Son Jesus Christ. The question is whether God's authority is accepted. If God is the maker of heaven and earth and our Creator, then it seems obvious that he is the source of right and wrong. If our world is a moral world, it is so because God made it so. If human beings are capable of making moral choices, it is because God so made humanity.

This is part of what Christians understand about God making men and women in his image. Part of that image is the capacity to make moral decisions. As Creator, God has given humanity certain patterns for life and we are meant to obey those norms. Part of being created means that we are answerable and responsible to God for what we do and how we live. The picture of the Garden of Eden tells us exactly that. Adam and Eve had been given certain standards to obey. They were not to eat of the forbidden fruit. They disobeyed and then God came to the garden and called to Adam. God wanted to know why Adam was hiding and what he had done. Adam was called in question by God. Humanity is answerable and responsible to God individually and as a community.

God's revelation of his standards and principles was clearly seen after humanity's fall and expulsion from the garden paradise. In a covenant relationship with Israel, God revealed his rules for living. If the people would obey these rules, then they would flourish and be blessed. If they disobeyed God's laws, then disharmony, destruction and God's curse would follow. The giving of God's laws comes in the covenant relationship, where God promises to be their God and keep his promises, while the Israelites also promise to obey God and do his will.

The giving of the Law, especially in the Ten Commandments,

clearly sets out the basic standards for the survival of any society. In the context of keeping a right relationship of worship to God, observing his day and honouring his name, God gives principles about parent–children relationships, truth-telling, sexual ordering in society, the value and sanctity of life, and attitudes to what belongs to individuals or groups. The laws given to Israel covered every aspect of living. God's rules concerned religious, social, community and ceremonial issues and situations.

Unfortunately, human capacity to obey God's Law was limited and human beings pleased themselves and did whatever was right in their own eyes. God's prophets were sent to recall his people to live as they were created to be. Again and again, the call of the prophets was to return to the original relationship with God and to live in the kind of ways which treated each other with justice and mercy. The teaching of the prophets and the wisdom literature in the Bible clearly express God's rules for living.

The incarnation of Jesus brought, Christians claim, God's full and final revelation. Jesus not only offered God's moral teaching – the Sermon on the Mount, the commandment to love one another as Christ loved, and the command to love one's enemies – he also lived out that morality. He embodied in flesh and blood and in the reality of human existence how human beings are to live. What he taught was shown in how he lived and died.

In Christian morality, there are principles at its heart, but the real meaning and truth of these principles are embodied in Jesus Christ. Of course, it is the case that different religions may come to different conclusions about moral matters, and there may also be vast measures of disagreement between those in any one religion. The Muslim world is divided into different sects, each of which claims that keeping its particular tradition is the only proper way to live. Jews too have different traditions which offer advice on moral issues, ranging from the orthodox to the liberal. Christianity is in exactly the same position, for Christians do not all reach the same conclusions about matters of morality. Quite clearly then, authority may provide answers to the issues but different authorities disagree and that very fact may introduce conflict for us.

The problem of authority is the problem of conflicting authorities. The only way to resolve such conflict is by finding an authority which is reliable and trustworthy. It is not enough for the authority to claim the right to be obeyed and accepted. That authority must have a proper and authentic right to our acceptance and obedience. In the conflict of authorities between the scribes and Pharisees on the one side and Jesus on the other, people recognized that Jesus taught not like the scribes and Pharisees, but as someone who had authority. True authority shows itself and so is trusted, accepted and obeyed.

It is no surprise, then, that people try to go behind the various religions and their claims to authority to some more basic account of morality. One such move, and a key one, is the *appeal to nature*. This argues that some things are good and others are bad because they are either natural or unnatural.

If we read much of the debate about homosexuality we discover how widespread this appeal to what is natural really is. Those who believe that homosexual practice is wrong argue that such behaviour is unnatural. Men and women are made for each other. Anatomically they fit together in a way which reveals that they are meant to go together. Biologically, they are required to have intercourse with each other in order to procreate. Children come into existence because men and women provide the basic material for the creation of new life. Any other sexual behaviour is held to be unnatural and perverted. It is a turning away from the natural order of things to engage in the unnatural.

Surprisingly, those who support alternative sexuality and its practice also use the same kind of argument. They suggest that those who are afraid of any kind of relationships with the same sex have failed to look sufficiently closely at what is natural. If they were more careful they would have discovered that the majority of people are attracted to members of the opposite sex and that is perfectly natural for them. But there is a substantial group of people – the estimates range from one in ten to one in twenty – who are genuinely and exclusively attracted to members of the same sex. For these people homosexual behaviour is the most natural thing in the world. Indeed, it is argued, for them to go to bed with the opposite sex would be quite *un*natural.

It is clear that both sides in a moral debate may appeal to what is natural. Nature may be used as the yardstick by which to judge moral issues. In modern moral philosophy, this approach is called *descriptivism*. It stresses that the way to resolve moral dilemmas is by a careful and accurate *description* of the real situation. The description will soon show that there are certain things which are good for people and certain other things which are bad for people. While this is not quite the same as the view that right is right because it is right and wrong wrong because it is the way things are, this description of right and wrong does seem to lead to the view that certain kinds of behaviour result in good results and other kinds in bad, because that is the way things are.

If I smoke forty cigarettes, drink three bottles of whisky and have four square meals a day, then my body will suffer. It was not designed to take that kind of punishment. That kind of behaviour leads to bad results. If I exercise regularly and eat and drink in moderation, then that leads to good results. Human beings are so constructed that certain ways of behaving and living are good for them. It helps them to flourish. Other ways of living and behaving are bad for us. Close attention to human nature and the way the world is and functions will show what is good and bad for us. This is the way the world is.

It is this idea that things are just like this, and there is nothing more to be said and nothing different to be done, which seems to be another way of expressing a morality based on nature. What is natural is the way things are, and we follow that way if we wish to flourish. If we fail to follow that way then we shall be in serious trouble. Christians argue that in making men and women and setting them in a created world, God expresses his moral nature and his moral laws, and makes the world and humanity moral.

The universe and the world we inhabit is not a morally neutral setting. It follows certain fundamental moral laws. There are certain patterns of cause and effect embedded in the way things are. The result is that we sow what we reap. One of the results of the tragedy of AIDS is that it has been a stark reminder that we live in such a world, where, if we abuse our bodies sexually or with drugs, we are at great risk from killer diseases. This is the way the world is, and it can offer us certain principles for living which it is foolish to ignore.

This is true not only about nature itself, but also about human nature. It is not good for us to be on our own all the time. While many of us may find coping with crowds of people difficult, we do, in fact, need other people. Those who have visitors in hospital get better more quickly than those who suffer from the same disease, but do not have anyone to come to see them. God has so created human beings and the world that there are things that are good and bad for us and it makes sense to discover what these things are.

Thus nature, what is natural and the way things are, does lie at the heart of this approach to morality. But it also recognizes that there is a positive benefit to be gained from following nature's guidance and direction.

Sometimes we are confronted with a slight variation on this theme. The clothes that young people wear and their general style of appearance often cause negative comment from the older generation. They argue that people don't usually go around like that. When we are behaving in ways which don't readily fit in with the rest of society, we are often accused of doing or being unusual. 'People don't do that sort of thing.' 'Where would we be if everyone did it?'

Often the kinds of arguments used by young people in response to this kind of attack are actually very similar. They say, 'But everyone my age does . . .'. Or they point to the way that all their friends are allowed to do this, so why shouldn't they be allowed as well? In other words, they are also appealing to what is usual and usually accepted. The only difference is that their frame of reference is a much smaller group of people like them. However, parents equally may be appealing to little more than a group of people who think and live exactly as they do. Both sets of people seem to be making an appeal to what is usually accepted and what society or a particular group in that society expects and requires. On this base, what is natural really means what is socially acceptable. What is socially acceptable is defined in terms of our crowd and peer group. Everyone else is abnormal and unnatural. It is by looking at what society does, that we learn what is right and wrong. Morality is obvious, if we only have the eyes to see it.

There are many other bases offered for the idea that right and wrong are obvious, self-defining and self-explanatory and need nothing else to defend or support them. But the one that is probably the most familiar to us is the notion of *conscience*. It is the natural inner sense of right and wrong. The history of morality has shown an emphasis on the importance of the conscience as a guide to morality. We know what is right and wrong because our conscience tells us.

Conscience works in two ways. First, it works *before* we do something. As we reflect on what we are about to do, conscience guides and directs. It seems to say that some things are good and right and other things are wrong and bad. Secondly, conscience works *after* the event. When we are tucked up safe and sound in bed, conscience is that inner voice which keeps us awake. It reminds us that we have done what we ought not to have done and we have failed to do what we ought to have done. Conscience seems to be an inner guide to what is right and wrong.

If we ask the question why we should do what our consciences tell us or how our conscience arrives at the conclusions it arrives at, some would reply, 'Because that is the way it operates and it just does get it right.' This is a variation on the theme 'What is right is right because it is right and what is wrong is wrong because it is wrong.'

In this way, making moral decisions is like looking at a puzzle made up of dots. The latest eye-test charts in the optician's consulting room have different coloured dots on a page. If your eyes are in good shape you are able to see that the dots actually make a number. Good eyesight means that we are able to discern patterns. When we hear a joke, sometimes we don't get the point immediately. But with a little helpful explanation from our patient friends, the penny eventually drops and we laugh, usually ten minutes after everyone else.

This seeing of the pattern or getting the joke is like a moment of intuition. In that moment, we know what we did not know before and see what before was obscure. Once we have seen it or know it, there is no need for any further explanation. We know it because it is obvious. We see it because it is crystal clear. In the same kind of way, this approach to moral decision-making, which rests in the idea that right and wrong are right and wrong in themselves and not for any other reasons we might offer, is like that moment of intuition. Listening to our conscience, looking at how society behaves or analysing what leads to human flourishing or harm can all be like a process of intuition.

When we are engaged in a moral argument and have exhausted all the arguments, we may come to the point where we want to say that the conclusion is obvious. Indeed, we may well feel that if other people do not understand what is right or wrong there is something wrong with them. Their moral sense is underdeveloped and faulty. What is really being suggested is that morality is a matter of all reasonable men and women coming to the same conclusions about what is right or wrong, as long as they are given all the facts. This last requirement is crucial, for failure on this point is used as the reason for a lack of unanimity about moral issues. The reason people reach different moral conclusions is that they are often dealing with different sets of facts. Moral discussion, therefore, is meant to take the form of giving other people the facts that they have overlooked and then waiting for them to arrive at the proper conclusion. If the description is faulty, then so will the morality be. The cure for moral disagreement is a fuller and better description.

There are thus a number of different possible sources for principles in morality, and the task of the moralist is to point to the correct sets of facts which will help us see the principles for themselves. If we do see them we will not need to do anything else. We shall not require any more convincing. These principles are self-evidently true. They are true in themselves and do not need any more support or justification. They are right because they are right or wrong because they are wrong. The other ground for principle morality is authority. Authority may present us with principles to be obeyed. But should we obey such authority?

Problems with principles

There are two main problems with any and every morality which seeks to rest on the basis of principles. At its simplest the first problem is, 'Where do we get our principles from? Whence are they derived?' The other main problem is 'How are we to cope with disagreement and difference?'

We saw how some people tried to base their morality on principles which are given by those in authority. This involves an implicit trust in and acceptance of what the particular authority says and sets up as the principles. The problem arises when we find that the authority in which we have invested so much may turn out to be mistaken or not quite what we expected or believed. Children are initially very shocked to discover that their parents do not know everything that there is to know and may even be wrong about certain things. It is quite common then to invest authority in someone else. The schoolteacher may be the source of authority, but it is soon evident that teachers are all too human and make mistakes too. Parents and teachers do not necessarily know best. The authorities we use as the basis of our principles may not always be absolutely right and may need to be questioned and checked from time to time.

But it is not only authority as the source of principles which runs into difficulties. Religions too may offer sources of principles. If I were an agriculturalist from the West sent out to an Indian village where the crops had failed and the people were facing starvation and death, and I discovered that there was in the village a large herd of cows, then I would be tempted to kill them for food for the population. The fact that there was no food to keep the cows alive and that they would die anyway would seem to support the desperate measure of killing the cows. The principle at stake would be the preservation of human life. To keep that principle I might be prepared to go to almost any length.

But if I were a Hindu resident in that village and was facing death from malnutrition and starvation, I would refuse to kill the cows. My religion would provide me with the principle that all life is sacred and that to take animal life is wrong even in order to save human life.

Religions thus present different principles which may well lead to conflict with each other as well as with other principles derived from elsewhere. We need to judge between the different authorities and religions and their competing moral claims. Which authority is to be accepted and obeyed?

It was suggested that conscience might be a source of principles and that we should always let our conscience be our guide. This seems like a good idea as long as our consciences are in good working order. But what is good working order for a conscience?

When I was still at school I went with a group of boys to the Edinburgh Festival. We were due to see a play and arrived long before the curtain was to go up. One older boy suggested that we visit the Quorum. There was general agreement, and I, thinking that this was some old Roman site, went along. It was a pub. I was horrified and refused to join them inside. I felt that a Christian ought not to go inside a pub. It never occurred to me that I could have had an orange juice and that Jesus was often to be found in settings where folks misunderstood what he was doing, but that in no way meant that he did anything wrong. My conscience was very sensitive, and looking back it seems that it was overdeveloped.

There was a time when I met many Christians whose

consciences seemed to be oversensitive and overdeveloped. But currently we seem to have swung to the other extreme. Nowadays people's consciences seem underdeveloped and insensitive. I remember a discussion with a group of young people from a Christian youth organization. The topic was how far it was proper for Christian young people to go in their relationships with the opposite sex. When I suggested that God might have certain standards which he required of all of us, there was general surprise. These young people seemed genuinely to think that what they did with their own bodies was their own business and nothing whatsoever to do with God. Their consciences seemed to me to be underdeveloped as Christian consciences. It is quite clear that there is a wide range of ground covered by the appeal to our consciences and that the principles we derive from these might not be quite so clear and self-evident as we would like and think.

Other people turn from conscience to the theme of what is natural as the basic ground and source of principles. Our earlier example of the debate about homosexuality and its practice in genital terms reveals something of the problem about the appeal to the natural. Those who believe that homosexual genital activity is unnatural argue that the male and female bodies are made for each other. They fit together. Biology reveals the natural order of things. Those who believe that homosexual activity is permissible between consenting adults argue that such behaviour is totally and utterly natural to those who engage in homosexual genital activity. Thus both sides in the debate make an appeal to the principle of what is natural, but end up with diametrically opposing views.

What makes the appeal to nature even more difficult for the Christian is that the world is a fallen world. Things now are not as they were meant to be or as they were created to be. Humanity went wrong and the whole order of reality was affected by that wrongdoing. Thus, when we look at nature as it is today, it is not necessarily how it was in the beginning. What is natural may be nasty, brutish and corrupting.

If we take this argument a stage further we realize that not only is nature not what it ought to be, but equally our grasp and understanding of what is natural may also be fallen and twisted. It is hard, then, to see how we can arrive at very much that is positive and crystal clear from the appeal to nature.

When you begin philosophy one of the earliest lessons is that you can have only one ultimate principle. If you have more than one ultimate principle there might arise a situation of conflict between these different principles. In such an event, it would be necessary to choose between the various principles. Inevitably, this would lead to some narrowing of principles until you were faced with a choice between the final two. Obviously only one could be held. This would be the fundamental principle at least for that moment – though it is hard to see how we could regard it as really being fundamental unless it was so not just for the moment but for some considerable time.

We have seen from the examination of the different sources of moral principles that the very variety of sources leads to different principles and thus to conflict between them. That is often the very heart of moral disagreement. It is the conflict between principles. Moral dilemmas are often the choices between different moral principles. What makes this all the more difficult is that the principles themselves do not tell us how we are to judge between these principles. Neither do the principles themselves tell us how to apply these principles to actual situations in real life. It is thus clear that different principles and sources of principles give rise to a complicated set of problems and conflicts. These disagreements constitute the second main difficulty with the use of principles as the sole basis of morality.

The different religious principles, different consciences, and different accounts of what is natural reveal the genuine and deep level of disagreement which there is between people. The problem with morality which appeals to certain principles is that it does not tell us how to solve disputes between differing principles.

The thrust behind such principle-based morality has often been that the moral decision-making is like a moment of intuition.

You are given all the facts and then when you look at them there comes a moment of insight. In that moment you know what to do without any hesitation. You know absolutely and certainly what is right and what is wrong. This sounds tremendously straight-forward, and it would be so if we all reached the same con-clusions. Sadly, it does not seem that we all have exactly the same situations. The cows in the Indian village and the debate over homosexual relationships show that when we are presented with the same evidence we still draw and apply different principles and these principles actually conflict with one another.

Intuition is rather a hit-or-miss affair. It is fine if you see it, but there are major problems if you do not. The most that can be said is that there is something wrong with your moral perception if you do not see what most normal moral people see. In fact, what we would do in such a case is to try to point to certain facts that may have been overlooked and seek to add to the descriptions already at work. This is a move to a more objective and rational account of morality.

Even this move may not solve the problem, however, for even if we are able to agree on the facts and accept the description, we may not be able to agree on the significance of the facts. We may fundamentally disagree about the significance of the facts and the values we attach to them.

In the end it seems that the approach to morality which stresses principles runs into various major problems. That does not mean that there are no principles or that there is nothing to be said based on principles. Rather it shows that morality based on principles alone is not enough. But if principles on their own are not enough, what is sufficient? It is here that we may turn to *consequences* as the ground and source of morality.

Chapter two

The end *justifies the means*

*A*ngela made an appointment to see me. Her problem was becoming obvious. She was pregnant. She was a student in her first year and she had been regularly sleeping with her boyfriend. They seemed to think that they were immune from the laws of nature, for they had not been using any contraceptive measures. When she discovered that she was going to have a baby, she visited her doctor and he had sent her, without any discussion, to the hospital to see the gynaecologist to arrange to have an abortion. The gynaecologist had asked her if it would make any difference if he tried to talk her out of having an abortion. She had said it would make no difference at all. He had said that in that case he wouldn't waste her time or his, and arranged for her to come in for her abortion.

Now she was not so sure, for she felt that if he had taken the time and trouble to talk to her about what abortion meant, she might well have changed her mind. So she wanted to look at the question with me.

She told me that the reason she was going to have an abortion was that the consequences of having the baby were too difficult for her to cope with. She did not want to marry her boyfriend now. He was going on to do research and marriage was out of the question. She was an only child and she did not want her parents to know what had happened. They had invested so much in their only daughter and were so proud of her. She couldn't let them down in that way. Besides, she argued, she was too young and immature to be a mother. She did not want a baby. She did not want the responsibility of bringing a child into the world. She couldn't face the thought of giving up her college career before it had really got going. Having this baby was out of the question and she would have to have an abortion. The consequences of going on with the pregnancy were too great.

Of course, she realized that she was not the only person involved in the decision. Nevertheless, she was quite clear that the boyfriend, friends and family had to leave the final decision to her. But what about the baby? There were consequences for the fetus in the womb. These consequences would be fatal. Angela knew that. She also knew that many women feel great guilt and unease after abortion. They can suffer from post-abortive trauma and that can affect their well-being for many years afterwards. She knew that there were consequences on both sides, but when she weighed the consequences that affected her directly against the others, she was sure that it was better to have the abortion than to have the baby.

Angela is typical of how we often go about the business of moral decision-making today. We are not so concerned about the principles at stake in any problem. We are very much more concerned about what will actually happen as a result of what we decide. *Consequences* are the basis for many moral decisions.

All you need is love

The Christian world has been deeply affected by this stress on consequences. Joseph Fletcher is an Anglican priest who has shaped much of modern Christian moral thinking. His view is often characterized in the words of the Beatles' song, 'All you need is love.' In his dismissal of a morality based on rules, principles and regulations, he wishes to avoid the other extreme of having no laws or rules at all. Rules do matter, but if love is better served by the abandoning of these rules then we must do the Christian thing. That is, in love to set aside the rules. This sounds like the heart of the gospel, and the only issue is how to describe what we mean by 'love'.

Fletcher offers a complex analysis of love, but it is clear that what he is actually offering is a morality of the possible. One of his key presuppositions is that of *pragmatism*. Fletcher is concerned to help us get things done. Already there is a hint here that what really matters is the end and not so much how we get there.

But Fletcher is honest as to what his view means. He offers six propositions which provide the content of 'situation ethics'. He calls his approach to decision-making 'situation ethics' because he believes that most morality fails to take the situation sufficiently seriously. What matters is what happens as a result of what you do. In detail this means that we should always seek to make sure that love is served by what is decided. This means that for Fletcher the end always justifies the means.

Many worldly thinkers have offered an analysis of morality which has suggested that it does not matter how you arrive at the final solution as long as you arrive at the correct place. This, of course, was and could be used to justify almost any atrocity on the way, as long as the end result was indeed good and satisfactory. Fletcher is not afraid to be honest about what his view means, for he knows that to give content to the notion of love means that we have to calculate what is loving in any situation. Love is calculating, according to Fletcher, and that means that we have to see if the consequences of what we decide and do are in the end loving or not. If the consequences are genuinely loving, then we must do it, even if it breaks the rules and means setting aside our principles. If the results are genuinely loving, then, indeed, the end has justified the means.

I had a friend who was a very young social worker. Her senior had given her a male client whose problems seemed to centre on a history of being dominated by the opposite sex. The man's wife and mother had mistreated him, and now he was ineffectual, inadequate and unable to function or relate properly to society. The senior explained that what was needed was a woman to 'give' herself sexually to the man with no demands, thus re-establishing his self-worth and value. He would then be freed from his negative self-image. His behaviour and attitude would change and all it needed was a self-sacrificing woman. Who better than this young social worker? My friend believed that the proper context for sexual expression is marriage and that adultery is wrong. She was challenged to set aside her principles and do the 'genuinely loving thing'. The end – one transformed client – would justify the means used to get there.

It is crucial for us to realize that this kind of approach to morality makes the consequences the central factor in any moral decision. What consequences will follow from what we do or fail to do? It is the results which count. What actually happens as a result of our decision thus becomes the criterion by which the goodness or badness of the decision ought to be judged.

It is not only what this stress on consequences implies about the nature of moral decision-making which is noteworthy. It also raises key questions about how we treat each other and the kind of dealings we ought to have with each other. At the centre of any moral view is some account of the attitudes we have towards another person and what is our understanding of the nature of a person.

Treating people as ends or means

There is a long history of the view that, whatever dealings we have with each other, we ought to treat each other as ends and not means. This is a shorthand way of saying that people must be treated with integrity as to whom and what they are in themselves. They are not to be treated as the means to some other end result or as pawns in some game in order to achieve our own ends. We must deal with each other without manipulating each other and using other people to get what we want. Treating others properly means taking their personality, desires and needs seriously and dealing with them in a just and equal fashion.

One of my main responsibilities is to teach medical ethics to medical and nursing students. To do that properly, one has to learn about what is happening in the medical world, especially in the realm of medical research. One area that is exercising the minds and hearts of many people inside and outside the medical and nursing professions is that of experimentation on fetal life. Those engaged in such research are genuinely concerned to have guidelines to help them know what is acceptable and permissible and what is not. Parliament and the legal profession are called into such discussions, as well as moralists. Some people have drawn a crucial line in the debate over the rights and wrongs of such experimental work. They would argue that it is right to experiment on a fetus only if the experiment or new, untried technique is for the good of that fetus. If the technique or experimentation is only for the good of others and has no direct benefit to the fetus, then it should not be permitted.

It is not surprising that many people disagree with this moral view, arguing that it is far too restrictive and that we need to do such experiments. They would argue that it is proper to conduct experiments on aborted fetuses, on fetuses which are going to be aborted anyway, and perhaps on embryos, or very early fetuses which have been produced as spare embryos in a fertility programme or even especially cultured for experimental purposes. This is the way forward to so many treatments, especially for infertility and hereditary diseases. Not all scientists would accept all of these categories, but it is the moral argument which goes with such views which is our concern here.

It is not only for the benefit of scientific understanding and pushing back the frontiers of knowledge that such experimentation is supported. It is argued that it is for the benefit of other fetuses which may be at risk from abnormality or early spontaneous abortion. It is the hope of developing genetic diagnosis and pre-natal care for other babies that may make it acceptable to conduct experiments on fetuses, even though the experiments will not help the fetuses directly or even in any way at all.

This is a clear example of how the fetus used in such experiments is not treated as an end in himself, herself or itself, but as a means to benefit others. Of course, this presupposes that such benefit will actually accrue, but that is not the point thus far.

Often a couple who have been married for a while may run into marital problems. They are not getting on very well with each other, so they talk to their families and friends about what they can do to make a difference. Some well-meaning people some-times suggest that they should start a family. Having a child will make all the difference in the world. It certainly will, though perhaps not quite in the way foreseen or intended. Having a child in order to shore up a failing marriage or as a means of solving a situation of marital conflict involves treating the child as a means to another end – saving the marriage. It is not treating the baby as an end in himself or herself, or bringing a child into the world as an end in itself.

The same pattern can be seen in the tragic situation of child sexual abuse. Often in these cases a parent sexually abuses the child for sexual satisfaction and as an instrument of selfish pleasure. It is not a responsible way of relating, but rather is using a helpless child as a means to the end of self-gratification.

This attitude of treating people as means to an end rather than as ends in themselves is a complicated affair. When it comes to sentencing criminals, the judge has to decide what sentence to give under what the law allows. Sometimes the judge tells the prisoner in the dock that he is being sentenced to a particularly severe punishment in order to make an example of him. It is hoped that such stiff sentencing will deter others from following in the criminal's footsteps. While we can see why this might happen, and even agree that it is a legitimate way for society to enforce certain laws and patterns of behaviour, it is also clear that there is a serious risk involved. We may end up treating the criminal in an unjust way, using him as a means of bringing about an important end, but not treating him for the crime he has done. In a sense he may be punished not so much for what he has committed as for what others might commit. Treating people as ends in themselves lies at the root of our understanding of justice.

Consequences and moral arguments

Behind situation ethics and this stress on using people as means to some other end lies an emphasis on *consequences* as the central and main feature of moral judgments. It is the results of our decisions which is the key to the morality of them. Good moral judgments are concerned with achieving good consequences and avoiding bad ones.

The way that this emphasis on consequences has dominated so much of our modern discussion of moral issues can be illustrated by looking at some modern moral debates and disagreements.

We live on the edge of nuclear war and holocaust. We have the capacity to destroy ourselves, each other and our world many times over. Yet we still earnestly debate the morality of nuclear weapons. One side argues that we must retain nuclear weapons because they are the ultimate deterrent against evil nations. We have these weapons to protect ourselves and to prevent the other side using their nuclear weapons to destroy us. Having such weapons is justified because it means that we protect our way of life, preserve our nation from slavery and the loss of our precious liberty, and ensure that our way of life continues and flourishes. In the end, the argument can come down to the belief that we need nuclear weapons in order to prevent certain unacceptable and unpleasant consequences. The end justifies the means.

Others vociferously oppose this view. The anti-nuclear groups argue that there is no justification for having nuclear weapons, even as a deterrent. The heart of their case often emphasizes the terrifying effects of nuclear weapons. They destroy people, animals and the very earth itself. Their use will make all life impossible. That is not just a short-term state of affairs. The use of nuclear weapons destroys the world for generations. Again, the stress is in exactly the same place as that of the pro-nuclear lobby. It is the consequences which make it so imperative that we should act in a particular way. Both sides in the debate seem to agree that it is consequences which ought to be the deciding factor. The problem for the undecided is which consequences we are to fear the most. Which consequences force us to one conclusion rather than another?

The debate around the growing use of technology and its ecological impact follows the same pattern. The one side argues that unless we allow technology to continue to grow and flourish we shall not find a solution to the immense problems that face us as individuals and as a world. To maintain our standard of living and combat disease and threats to human existence we must develop yet more technological skill and expertise.

The contrary view looks at the impact of modern technology on our environment and on our humanity. The argument stresses the pollution and destruction of our air, water and land resources. We are running out of earth, and, if we continue on this pathway, we shall destroy ourselves and make the world a wilderness where no-one can survive.

Both sides, again, are in the business of drawing our attention to the consequences of the decisions we make. If we did but appreciate the significance of these consequences properly, then we would be sure to make the right decisions about what to do now. Morality is all about the consequences which result from the decisions we make. Right and wrong are decided by the results.

There is a prudential streak in all this. It sounds like someone giving us advice to do such-and-such a thing because in the end it is in our own best interests. We are told to give aid to the Two Thirds World, for if we do not, if and when the balance of power and resources shifts in their favour, they will refuse to help us just as we are in danger of refusing them aid now.

Our world faces a catastrophe as a result of the spread of AIDS. Governments have been forced into major publicity campaigns in order to drive home the seriousness of the crisis facing us all. Yet the emphasis in these adverts, commercials and publicity is that we are to pursue safe sex. The warning is clear. If we do not take precautions to try to achieve safer sex, then we will be at risk of catching AIDS. The argument is purely prudential. It appeals to what we should do in our own best interests. It threatens us with certain unpalatable consequences if we fail to take precautions. There are many causes of moral unease about the campaign, but for the moment let us focus on the fact that the central point at issue is a matter of consequences. Act in one way to avoid certain consequences. Acting in another way is guaranteed to put each of us at risk and may well lead to terrifying and fatal consequences. Morality, on this view, is just a matter of consequences. Right and wrong are determined by the results of what we choose and do or fail to do.

It is hard to underestimate the all-pervasive emphasis on consequences which lies at the heart of our current moral thinking, arguing and discussion. But will this do as an adequate account of the nature of morality? Is this sufficient as a basis for a moral way of living?

Problems with consequences

If we reflect a little on the situation we have reached in examining this emphasis on consequences, we shall realize that there is often an implicit appeal to selfishness and self-interest behind many of the arguments we have looked at. It is in our own best interests to do this or that. But is that all there is to morality? It looks as if to accept consequences as the sole ground for moral decision-making is to believe that self-centredness and selfishness are the sum total of morality. This seems far from being the case, and no matter what the consequences of any action are likely to be we can still always ask whether or not that is a good or a bad, right or wrong, thing for us to do. Even if the consequences may be very bad for us personally or communally, there may be things which it is right to do and other things which are always wrong for us to do. Morality is more than just consequences.

But even if it were only a matter of consequences we would still have major problems. The first would be that we would still have to have some kind of system for choosing between consequences.

How can we decide whether or not it is better to be 'red' than dead? Whether ecological risk is more or less important than technological discovery and application? Consequences alone will not tell us which set of results are more to be feared and which ones we ought to aim for.

There is, however, a more fundamental flaw in this stress on consequences. I am a fellow of an Oxford college and our college is led by a Warden, who acts as Principal. Imagine a scenario in which I have a lifelong, burning ambition to become Warden of the college. One day I am walking down the street outside our college with the Warden, when I am suddenly overcome by this desire to be the Warden. I lose control and give the current Warden a loving friendly push into the middle of the road where cars and buses are whizzing past at an alarming rate.

At that precise moment, providence intervenes to preserve the life of the Warden. The driver of the nearest bus has a mild heart attack and loses control of his bus so that he swerves. In swerving, he misses the Warden who is lying in the middle of the street. Sadly, the bus mounts the pavement and knocks me down instead. (These everyday stories usually have happy endings, but the nearest happiness for me would be that the funeral orations would be splendid to hear.) To the casual observer, the scene is one in which this brave little Scotsman saves the life of the Warden of the college. He pushes him out of the way of the careering bus and takes the full force of the crash himself, thus fatally injuring himself. This is not quite an accurate account of what was happening. In reality I was trying to kill the Warden, but I could neither predict nor control the consequences of my actions.

Therein lies the main objection to any and every morality which seeks to base itself on consequences alone. We cannot predict or control the consequences of our own actions, far less other people's actions. We cannot control everything that will happen in the world, and the best we can hope for is some kind of probability. There is more to morality than consequences alone.

This is partly why people are uneasy about treating others as means to an end rather than ends in themselves. Justice and fairness seem to require more from our dealings with each other than manipulation and abuse. The stress on consequences does not deal with all the moral dimensions of issues. Indeed, it is not without its own problems.

The situationist seems to offer a cure to our moral problems, but, ignoring his use of extreme cases which always lead to bad laws, he does not tell us how to define a situation. He is not clear when a situation is to begin or come to an end so that we can calculate the consequences properly. The danger will be that we do the calculation too soon.

This was exactly what happened in relation to the contraceptive pill for women. After many trials it was pronounced safe, and women in the West were prescribed it and used it, confident that relief from the likelihood of pregnancy was a great gain with no risks attached. The truth of the matter became clear only later when the risks in terms of heart problems became evident and the search for a safer pill began. The consequences in the short term may have seemed good and positive, but in the long term they were not so positive, and were even fatal in some cases. It is not clear how long we have to judge the consequences of some action or event. No matter how long we wait, the benefits of hindsight may not make any difference to those adversely affected before.

We are in danger of misleading, for consequences *are* important and it is vital that, as far as we are able, we do try to foresee what the consequences will be. Many commentators use such an argument based on consequence as a proper warning of the dangers we may face. They argue that if we adopt a particular policy we may be on a slippery slope and end up in a place where we do not wish to go.

When the abortion law was introduced to Great Britain in 1967, most doctors felt that it would allow only abortions which were clearly required. The reality has been very different, for it has resulted in abortion on demand rather than relief for the few at risk. People were given an inch and took a mile. The slippery slope operated, and many feel that it is better never to open the door to such things than to end up in such a terrible state. Rightly, this view emphasizes the importance of consequences, even if it is extremely pessimistic about our capacity to limit those consequences and to frame laws which would ensure that only what we wish to be allowed is allowed and that the rest continues to be forbidden.

Christian morality is quite clear that consequences do matter. The behaviour of humanity in the days of Noah led to the Flood. Again and again the Israelites misbehaved and this led inevitably to tragic consequences. If we live in certain ways, then the consequences will be disastrous. If we lived as God intends, then blessing flows, and follows. Naturally, such consequences are not to be the motivation for doing what is right and good. We ought not to be frightened into being good simply to avoid hell. We cannot be forced into goodness merely in order to gain a front seat in the heavenly choir. Neither would be genuine goodness.

But we will and do find that consequences are a crucial part of Christian morality. How we live and what we do have inevitable consequences, which give great significance to how we behave. Our living here and now affects not only the results in the here and now. Life after death will be quite different in the light of our behaviour in the present.

There are two particularly chilling examples in the pages of the gospels. The first is the parable of Dives and Lazarus (Luke 16:19–31). Dives – the rich man – lived in luxury, while Lazarus, a poor beggar, suffered at the gates of the rich household. In death, Lazarus was taken to Abraham's bosom – a Jewish understanding of paradise. Dives was in hell – the place of fire. He longed for Lazarus to cool his tongue with a drop of water. But the gulf was too great. Dives had put himself beyond help by his carelessness and lack of love. When he was able to help Lazarus, Dives had done nothing. The consequences of his failure were terrifying.

That is exactly the thrust of Jesus' picture of the judgment of the nations in Matthew 25. Men and women will be judged by what they did or failed to do to the needy. Those who put love into action will be rewarded. But for those who failed to see and seize the opportunities, the condemnation is aweful. 'Depart from me, you who are cursed, into the eternal fire prepared for the devil and his angels. For I was hungry and you gave me nothing to eat, I was thirsty and you gave me nothing to drink, I was a stranger and you did not invite me in, I needed clothes and you did not clothe me. I was sick and in prison and you did not look after me' (Matthew 25:41–43). Christianity is quite clear that what we do and fail to do matter not only in their immediate but also in their long-term consequences.

Consequences do matter in morality, but the totality of a moral judgment needs to be noted. A moral decision is made up of the motives at work, the principles involved, the nature of the action done, and the results of consequences. All of these together make up a moral action, and to do justice to morality we have to consider what motives and aims are at work, what principles are being used as guidelines and standards, what kind of moral action is involved and whether or not the means being used are good or bad, as well as what probable and likely consequences will follow from what is done. Morality is not just a matter of consequences.

Chapter *three*

Eat, *drink and be merry*

'*E*at, drink and be merry for tomorrow we diet.' This play on the old adage about eating, drinking and being merry, for tomorrow we all die, sums up the spirit of the current age. Some would say that this is the spirit of every age. We all live for pleasure.

Traditionally this approach to life has been called *hedonism*. Behind such hedonism is really a self-centred approach to life. This self-centredness is one part of the concern about things turning out well and ending up with good consequences which we saw is so much part and parcel of modern moral debate and discussion. But the hedonist or the ethical egoist, who believes that morality is really about selfishness, goes further. He argues that what we do, we *want* to do. This becomes an approach to moral decision-making when we move from 'This is the way we actually are' to the view that 'This is the way we *should* be.' A description has become a prescription.

In other words, it suggests that we should do what we want and that there is nothing at all wrong with that as a philosophy and approach to life. The only issue at stake is what it is that we really want. The person faced with the temptation to blow all his savings on a trip to Hawaii may well give in to that temptation and thus do what he wants. But the virtuous person may struggle to resist the temptation of the beaches and sunshine and overcome his desire. Nevertheless, it is argued, he does what he wants. The fact that he overcomes the temptation and settles for keeping his savings and an easy conscience shows that these things are actually what he wanted. We all do what we want in the end.

But that still leaves us with the question of what it is that most of us want. What we do want is to be happy. We want to be satisfied and fulfilled, and to enjoy ourselves. This means that pain and pleasure are the real bases of morality. On this view, we judge what is right and wrong by the pleasurable consequences which result or the bad consequences we avoid.

This can mean only that psychologically this is the way people are. It is thus an account of what motivates people to act or refrain from acting. Pleasure turns them on, so they do what leads to pleasurable results and avoid what is painful.

When our sons were much smaller, we used to regulate their behaviour by the threat of punishment. To give them time to think about whether or not they really wanted to be smacked and to ensure that we did not hit them out of anger and lose control of ourselves, we would begin to count up to three. We found that rarely, if ever, did we reach the magic number of three. The warning and the time to reflect on what pain would ensue were quite enough to stop the bad behaviour and ensure that something like good manners prevailed. They acted as they did, not out of some great moral motivation, but out of sheer selfishness and self-preservation. To avoid pain and maintain their pleasure, they did as they were told.

The hedonist argues that this is what we all do. We learn what leads to pleasure and happiness and what results in painful experiences. We seek what brings pleasure and avoid what brings pain.

Some go a stage further and suggest that not only is this what we actually do, but that it is also what we *ought* to do. In trying to live a morally good life, people ought to seek pleasure. This is how we should live as individuals and as a society.

The 'greatest happiness' principle

One problem with this emphasis on hedonistic pleasure is that it could lead to the disintegration of society. If all of us did whatever turned us on, and if that was not the same for everyone, we would end up at each other's throats in social anarchy. Whether it is what we eat, where to spend the evening, what to see, how to dress, which political party to vote for, or just how to live our everyday lives, it is quite clear that much of the conflict in our society stems from very different ideas of what will please and satisfy us. Jeremy Bentham and John Stuart Mill realized this. They created the view called *utilitarianism*.

When governments in the West decide on particular policies and pursue them actively, what lies behind such policies and execution? Mill and Bentham argued that it was the idea of the *greatest happiness of the greatest number*. We make our practical, social, political and moral decisions on the basis of what will lead to the greatest happiness of the greatest number.

Once a year the local Health Authorities at a regional level have to allocate their budgets for the different areas of health care. In order to do that they use a complex formula which tries to calculate how much happiness will result by spending money on one area rather than on another one. They look at the numbers affected, the likely benefits to them, the cost, the potential drawbacks, and the spin-off benefits, and then arrive at judgments about whether to spend more money on the care of the elderly or on kidney dialysis and heart transplantation. The aim and basis for the decision-making are clearly what will lead to the greatest happiness of the greatest number.

Inevitably, this depends on having some kind of calculus, and Bentham realized this from the start. He knew that for this view to work, he would need to measure pleasure. He therefore designed a 'pleasure calculus'. It tries to measure the pain and the pleasure in each and every situation. If there is a surplus of pain over pleasure, then we ought to do what leads to more pleasure. If there is more pain than pleasure as a result of our decision-making, then we should stop what we are doing and reverse the process. Morality is all about the calculation of pleasurable and painful consequences.

Bentham's calculus asks about the duration, intensity, propinquity (closeness), extent, certainty, purity and fecundity (fruitfulness) of pleasure and pain. He suggested that when we are faced with a moral choice we should ask how long the pleasure will last and how intense and satisfying it will be. Obviously, the longer the better, and the more intense the more it is to be desired. Pleasures which are nearer and affect more people are better than those which are more distant and affect only a few people. We should pursue the pleasures which, we know beyond all reasonable doubt, will actually happen, rather than merely clutching at unlikely straws.

The purity of the pleasure is important. This was brought home to me on a visit to the Open University at Keele. Part of the work of the Open University is to expose its mature students to a wide cultural experience. Part of this was achieved by showing them dramatic performances which most of us might never get a chance to see. One evening we were to be shown a film of *A Midsummer's Night Dream*. It starred James Cagney and Mickey Rooney. With the other staff, I was sitting at the back of the theatre. The film began and Cagney said something and we all laughed. He acted or hammed away and we laughed and laughed. Rooney came on and we were helpless with laughter. After twenty minutes I thought that if I did not get a grip and stop laughing I would be in serious trouble. Then Cagney and Rooney would do something else and off I would go again. By the end of the film I was writhing in agony in my seat. The pleasure was not a pure pleasure. It was more than a little tinged with pain. We ought to look for pure pleasures, argued Bentham, and not pursue those which are mingled with pain.

The final point on the calculus is fecundity: whether this particular pleasure is merely a one-off pleasure, or whether it will lead to more of the same kind. We ought to follow the kind that leads to more of a good thing, the argument goes, rather than an isolated pleasurable experience.

By adding up the pleasure which will result in any situation and subtracting from that total the amount of pain that will result, it is possible, according to Bentham, to arrive at a positive or negative total of pleasure. If there is a positive amount of pleasure we ought to do that. If there is a negative amount, then we ought to avoid doing that.

Our task is not a detailed discussion of the merits of utilitarianism, but a series of major criticisms were offered. Mill took on the mantle to try to save the theory, and sought to draw a distinction between the *quantity* and the *quality* of the pleasures. This was a direct response to the charge that utilitarianism was a 'doctrine fit for pigs'. Bentham had encouraged that interpretation of the philosophy by stressing that, if the quantity of pleasure was the same, then playing on a pinball machine was just as good as reading poetry. Mill tried to produce a distinction between different kinds of pleasure, and argued that quality was important. It was better to be Socrates dissatisfied than a pig satisfied. Cultural and aesthetic pleasures were more important than simple bodily lusts.

Mill also introduced a principle of justice or equity to make the theory a more balanced and practical one in which the rights of the individual could be preserved more easily. Whether or not he was successful in saving the theoretical basis of the philosophy, it is certainly the case that utilitarianism is alive and well in our world in practice.

There is wide appeal in the idea of pleasure and its measurement as a means of reaching social and political answers to the problems that face us as a society. The truth of the matter is that most democratic governments operate on a utilitarian base. They are concerned with the greatest happiness of the greatest number, realizing that there is an election just around the corner and the party returned to power will be the party which pleases the voters most. To examine utilitarianism is not to play a philosophical game. It is to look at the realities of political decisions. Social morality, like the personal morality described by the hedonist, is a matter of seeking pleasure and avoiding pain. Happiness is the name of the moral game.

Problems with pleasure

In the last chapter we tried to show that any and every morality which depended on consequences alone ran into major problems. Hedonism and utilitarianism run into those same problems. Both theories rely totally on the consequences of our actions and use those consequences as the basis for morality. Thus difficulties about predicting and controlling consequences, as well as the awareness that, even when all the consequences have been totalled and counted, it is still possible to ask whether what is to be done is right or wrong, reveal the inadequacy of 'teleological' (or consequential) theories. There is more to morality than such a stress on consequences alone.

But the emphasis on pleasure has other difficulties as well. The hedonist makes morality a matter of selfish interest. It is literally 'pleasing myself'. All that seems to matter on this view is that I make sure I look after number one. Other people are important only in so far as they impinge on my own happiness.

Yet this seems to contradict what most of us think about morality. All too often the crunch comes in a moral dilemma when we realize that what we want will not do in this situation. If I witness a mugging, I may not want to get involved. But I have a responsibility to help, even if I don't want to get caught up in that situation. We have to do our duty. We have to do what is right. I may be in a setting where telling a lie is the easiest way to blame someone else and get myself off the hook. To tell the truth will certainly bring pain for me rather than pleasure. But morally we have to avoid what is wrong, even if it is pleasurable. Morality often seems like a way of saying 'No' to ourselves rather than pursuing our own pleasure.

The hedonist would protest that in saying 'No' to myself I am really doing what gives me pleasure and what I actually want to do. The problem with this response is that it destroys all sense of the notion of 'wanting' and 'pleasure'. Everything I do becomes what I want. Everything I choose is what gives me pleasure simply by the fact that I choose and do it.

Most of us know perfectly well the difference between doing what we want to do and doing what we ought to do. No amount of hoping that in the end it will make us happier changes the genuine pain and loss of pleasure which we face in making a hard choice. In his most famous film, *Brief Encounter*, Trevor Howard meets a woman at a railway station and they fall in love even in such a short space of time. They are tempted to build on the new relationship and to forget all about their responsibilities to other people and the other relationships they have. To do that would possibly bring them both happiness on a scale they have not known before. Nevertheless, they both know that such a step would be wrong, and they agree to part. There is a real sense in which what they are doing gives them pleasure. Selfishness would have dictated that they begin an affair. Duty, responsibility and morality decree something quite different.

The hedonist account runs into a further problem if we begin to analyse what actually gives people pleasure. To illustrate the difficulty, I remember being told a joke about a sadist and a masochist. The masochist says to the sadist, 'Beat me. Beat me.' The sadist says, 'No.' The masochist wants the pleasure of having pain inflicted on himself. The sadist wants something different. He wants to hurt people, but he certainly doesn't want to please them. To cause a masochist pain means refraining from giving him pain. But we don't need to be sadists or masochists to know that different people want and desire different things. Different people gain pleasure from very different things, and that will inevitably lead to conflict. The emphasis on pleasure does not tell us how to resolve disagreements over pleasure and conflicts of interest. Instead of a recipe for moral decision-making, we are given a recipe for conflict and anarchy. Morality is not just about pleasure.

As we have already said, even when we discover what it is that gives us pleasure and makes us happy, it is always possible to reflect on the morality of seeking to fulfil those sets of desires. This seems clearly to distinguish morality from pleasure and pain.

However, we must not claim too much here. What brings pleasure and pain is a part of our moral reflection, and does affect what we decide to do and refrain from doing. The 'good news' of Jesus was that he brought salvation and abundant life. Jesus came in order to bring people into true happiness. True happiness is to be found in a proper relationship with God.

One visiting preacher was to be met at the railway station and did not know who was to meet him. The person waiting likewise did not know the visiting preacher. After waiting until almost everyone had gone he approached one man with the question. 'Are you the visiting preacher?' The reply was, 'No, it's indigestion that makes me look like this.' So often that is our picture of Christianity. It can seem such a sad, killjoy affair, always negative.

But even if the church must plead guilty to failing to show the joy and happiness of life in Christ, it is certainly clear from the pages of the Bible that only in relationship with God do human beings find true fulfilment and happiness. Christian morality is concerned with happiness now and in the future. However, this cannot be the motive for morality. If I'm good only to get a reward or to avoid punishment, that is nothing but sheer selfishness and self-interest. Happiness and genuine satisfaction are the natural and inevitable results of living as we are meant to live in harmony with God and so with each other. Happiness, in biblical terms, is not just a vague feeling. It is being a whole person in harmony with God, each other and the world around us. *Shalom*, or wholeness, is what Christian morality leads to for us all. Pleasure and happiness are an integral part of Christian morality, for they are part of our humanity.

Like the stress on consequences, the emphasis on pleasure and pain points to our human concerns and the things that *do* us good as well as what *is* good. The danger is always of reducing the complexity of morality simply to one aspect. There is more to morality than a mere concern with pleasure and pain.

The utilitarian account of morality suffers from these criticisms but also runs into one or two more of its own. It suggests that moral decisions should be based on the results of a pleasure–pain calculation. The problem is whether or not pleasure and pain are really the kinds of things that can be measured at all. The pleasure one son gets from hearing that Scotland have won a football international against England cannot easily be added to my pleasure at seeing him happy. Nor can it be easily joined with the pleasure he gets from eating a bar of chocolate as the game proceeds. Pleasures are not easy to add together, whether they are all individually felt or between people.

Even more difficult is to talk of subtracting pain from pleasure. While one son rejoices at the Scottish victory, the other is thrown into the depths of despair that his favourite English team has been beaten. What kind of sum is it that measures the pain and pleasure in each case and then somehow or other adds or takes the one away from the other? Pleasure is not easily calculated. Nor are pain and pleasure of equal concern. If we are given a choice between helping someone in agony or enjoying ourselves for a brief moment, we would surely agree that we ought to help the person in agony. The relief of pain seems more important than the creation and pursuing of positive pleasure.

Despite Mill's attempts to the contrary, there does seem to be a conflict between the idea of simply calculating the amount and quantity of pleasure and trying to have some system for estimating the quality of pleasure. How we can really compare listening to the Beatles with reading the latest Frederick Forsyth novel seems problematic to say the least. Obviously qualitative judgments do happen and are important, but how we actually do the calculation seems more complicated than even Mill's revised account of utilitarianism allows. His attempt to save the theory in fact only makes explicit a fundamental tension within the theory, which detracts from its apparent simplicity and thus its practical value.

This raises the question of complexity and the degree to which the utilitarian theory actually provides us with a workable way of coping with decisions. There are genuine political and social matters involved even if there seems to be more to morality than is suggested here. But the complexity makes the theory less helpful than it appears to be. This is also revealed when we consider another major problem in the theory.

When I started teaching, I was given the advice to be kind to students. As you will see, this created unexpected problems, but it also makes term-time a pain. All the time, I try to keep students happy. The vacation breaks come as a great relief, for they mean that I can please myself. One of the things that make me happiest is the sound of my own voice, especially to a captive audience. When I am invited to speak at a conference I am delighted. Here is another opportunity to please myself. The problem is that they usually give me only an hour or an hour and a half. In this example, it is important that the reader realizes that I am a deeply sensitive human being and that accordingly my capacity for pain and pleasure is enormous. So when I am invited to speak at a conference I try to calculate the amount of pleasure that I will derive from having the audience listen to me for an hour. I soon realize that I could have far more pleasure if they listened to me for four hours. So I quickly do the sum and end up with an enormous amount of pleasure, which we shall call $50x$ of pleasure.

I am not just deeply sensitive, but also a rational person. I recognize that after three and a half hours – certainly not before – one, or at the most two, of the audience will be experiencing a certain degree of pain and physical discomfort. This will probably be in the posterior region. But even when I calculate the amount of pain that an audience of one hundred people will feel on listening to my lecture for four hours, it comes to the meagre total of $6x$ of pain. On the basis of this calculation of the greatest happiness, I announce that I shall lecture for four hours. This is obviously the right thing to do, for there is $44x$ more pleasure as a result of the extension of my lecture. Sadly, this is not always as popular a suggestion as one would expect. People complain that it is not fair. They tell me that it is unjust and that there are far more of them than there is of me.

Mill saw the point behind the criticism, and introduced the

principle of justice or equity. He argued that everyone should count for one and no-one for more than one. This was designed to prevent us doing what the over-sensitive want all the time. It raised, however, the implicit tension between the greatest amount of happiness and the greatest number of people. Justice requires that each person has only one vote or say in the calculation. The problem is that the alleged simplicity and directness of utilitarianism disappears and pleasure itself is no longer the sole base. Mill is implicitly recognizing that there is more to morality than pleasure and happiness.

Unfortunately, his so-called cure may not help us out of our moral difficulties either. It we agree that everyone counts for one and no-one for more than one, then we may end up doing what the Chinese want all the time, because there are more of them than of the rest of us. If we accept Mill's solution, we end up with the tyranny of the majority. That may be equity, but it is certainly not necessarily justice. The rights of the few need to be safeguarded in any and every setting where the majority view carries the day. Morality requires some fair dealings and protection for the few, even when their outlook may run counter to that of the majority of a society.

Our analysis shows that there are many difficulties with an attempt to make pleasure and happiness the ultimate basis of morality. But it is not just that it seems impossible to construct a pleasure-based moral theory. It is also that such a theory fails to do justice to the nature of morality in all its complexity. Pleasure and pain, happiness and fulfilment are part of our moral outlooks and human nature, but that is very far from making them the core of morality.

Chapter *four*

Everything *is* relative

*W*hen I came down from the Holy Land of Scotland to the sophisticated setting of England I was given a helpful piece of advice. If I wanted to be a success as a lecturer, then the secret was to be nice to students. Within a few days I met my first student, who happened to be a near neighbour. I remembered the advice and thought how best to be nice to him. I decided that the best I could do for him was to invite him to my home to taste my wife's excellent cooking. He was delighted, and, when he explained that he was married, the invitation was extended to them both.

Ere long the day of the dinner party dawned and the evening came. The doorbell rang and we went to greet our guests. I introduced the student to my wife. He then kissed my wife. In the part of Scotland I come from, when someone else kisses your wife, you smash him in the face. I did, however, realize that this was not quite the way to begin, far less maintain, a deeply meaningful, ongoing relationship, so I restrained myself. I quickly discovered that this behaviour was not uncommon among the English. In social settings it soon became obvious that it was perfectly proper to kiss other people's wives by way of greeting. Now, after many years in the deep south, I am just about able to behave like everyone else. I have had to learn that when I am in Rome, I am supposed to do as the Romans do.

Imagine a tribe in North Africa who hold a very particular set of beliefs. They believe that after death we carry on a journey in the same state as we leave the present life. It would be no surprise, then, to find that, if one of their near relatives was in danger of becoming frail and a little decrepit, they would kill and eat him so as to send him on to the next world in a hale and hearty condition. If, in contrast, we were to observe the cultural behaviour in the south of England, we would find that when the elderly begin to show signs of frailty, they are put into an old folks' home to be properly looked after and cared for. So it appears that there are different rules in different places.

This outlook produces a particular brand of morality which is called *ethical relativism*. It is the notion that what is right and wrong, good and bad, varies. These ideas vary from time to time, person to person and place to place. In other words, there are no absolute standards of morality. There are no moral principles which are always true at all times and in all places. Morality varies according to the context. Different times, places and people come up with very different attitudes to moral issues. What is right and wrong depends on where and what you are. One quotation sums up this view pithily.

> It all depends on where you are,
> It all depends on when you are,
> It all depends on what you feel,
> It all depends on how you feel.
> It all depends on how you're raised,
> It all depends on what is praised,
> What's right today is wrong tomorrow,
> Joy in France, in England sorrow,
> It all depends on point of view,
> Australia or Timbuctoo,
> In Rome do as the Romans do.
> If tastes just happen to agree
> Then you have morality.
> But where there are conflicting trends,
> It all depends, it all depends . . .
>
> A. Edel in *Ethical Judgement: The Use of Science in Ethics* (Glencoe, Illinois: The Free Press, 1955)

This outlook towards moral issues is very much taken for granted in our pluralistic world. We all live in the midst of difference. In our great cities there are many different racial and religious groups. They dress, live, eat, bury and marry in a wide variety of ways. Different cultures are constantly coming in contact with each other and having to live side by side. But there are genuine and fundamental problems over different attitudes to everything, from education and child-rearing to the roles of men and women and the kind of food and drink which is normal and acceptable.

Popular travel, and the shrinking of the world we experience when television brings events from all over the globe into our living rooms, has meant that we are constantly confronted by different cultures, attitudes and moral outlooks. The very presence of difference raises questions about how we live and cope with disagreement over moral issues. One standard response is to argue that moral values are relative and vary from time to time, place to place, and person to person.

The popular way of expressing this belief is that you can do your thing, as long as I am free to do my thing, whatever it happens to be. Whatever turns each and every one of us on is acceptable. But the relativist realizes that if each of us did whatever was right in his own eyes and pursued his own way of living and his own personal moral standards, society would be in danger of disintegration and collapse. Our desires and standards would inevitably conflict with each other, and we would soon need some system for coping with conflict and disagreement.

The relativist has an answer for this problem. He suggests that the cure for the problem of fundamental disagreement is *tolerance*. You are free to do your thing only and in so far as I am free to do my thing. We are able to live together with our differences as long as we are prepared to tolerate each other and our different moral views. 'Live and let live' is the motto for a society that wishes to prevent disintegration and collapse.

Relativism leads almost inevitably to tolerance. The easiest way of coping with variety and difference is simply to accept the differences and allow every view to be held with equal standing. Every moral view is just as good as every other one. Tolerance is the way for a society to preserve itself and for people to live in harmony even when they hold contrasting moral attitudes and beliefs. After all, the relativist claims, there are no absolute, universal standards or norms.

Everything is relative, relatively speaking

The first and the most fundamental problem with the philosophy of relativism is how it may be stated as a philosophy at all. If I argue that everything is relative, is the statement that everything is relative an absolute or a relative statement? If it is an absolute statement and I am really saying that absolutely everything is relative, then it is not true. In making that statement I am falling into a fatal contradiction. In saying that everything is relative, I am, in fact, producing one absolute statement. That statement is that everything is relative.

What this argument reveals is that there are some views which are literally self-contradictory. When we try to say what they are, the very act of saying, and the words we use to state the view, cancel out what is being said. To make a claim about everything is an absolute claim, and, if it is correct, it shows that there is at least one absolute thing that can be said. The problem for the relativist is that he wants to deny that there are such absolute, universally true things. When he tries to describe his view that there are no such absolutes he falls into the inevitable trap of using a universal and absolute statement to try to make his point.

For some strange reason, people often imagine that this kind of argument is typical of philosophers, who are simply playing with words. The complaint has some justification, for it is certainly a playing with words, but it is not only that. It draws attention to a fatal problem for some philosophies and attitudes. The very words we use to try to state them lead inevitably to self-contradiction. But it is not only that such views cannot be stated. They cannot be believed or put into practice without falling into contradiction. The relativist runs into fatal problems as he tries to state, believe and live his philosophy, for he literally contradicts himself and rules out what he says by what he says.

Of course, there is another course open to the relativist. In response to the query about whether his statement of his position is absolute and universal or not, he may maintain that it is only relatively true. That naturally implies that it is only true at some times for some people in some places. This would certainly be much more consistent with the nature of what is being claimed. If all truth is only relatively true, then the truth that all truth is only relatively true, must itself be relatively true.

There is, however, a price to be paid for this way of avoiding the charge of inconsistency. It is that relativism becomes merely one view alongside the myriad of others. It is perfectly open for anyone and everyone to respond that, if it is true only for some people at some times in some places, it need not be true as far as they are concerned. Relativism seems to lead to every view being of the same worth and value as every other view, if it is consistent within a particular context. But if it is only relatively true, then it does not pose the threat to morality that it seems. It is simply one view alongside all the others.

Facing the facts

There is an equally damning criticism of moral relativism which deals another fatal blow to it. It is not true. Relativism argues that moral standards vary from time to time, place to place and person to person. There are no absolute, universal moral standards. But there are. If we were to examine the whole wealth of moral codes from all the great religious and legal and ethical settings across the cultures and down through history, we might expect to see endless variety. In fact, we would find that there is a common core of morality. This common core reveals an astonishing degree of unanimity about the nature of morality.

Every legal, moral and religious code contains some kind of rule or regulation about truth-telling. When it is required to tell the truth and when, and under what circumstances, it might be permitted to tell lies, is basic to morality. Likewise, every moral code has some kind of restriction on sexual behaviour. At its crudest, it often describes whom one is permitted or forbidden to take as a sexual partner. There is always some kind of regulation based on the sanctity of life. It usually takes the form of who may be killed and when. This also implies that there are others who may not be killed and whose lives are to be protected. There are similar rules about parents and children. That parents are to be respected and obeyed seems to be a universal value. The final standard which seems to be universal deals with what is mine or ours and what is not mine or not ours. Some have interpreted this as some universal value attached to property, but the danger is that we have too narrow a view of property. It is rather a morality of what belongs, and therefore what is to be defended, and what does not belong. Of course, there may be conditions under which it is to be taken and made to belong, but even that reveals a standard of what originally belonged and what did not.

What is fascinating about these universal norms is that they form part of God's Ten Commandments. They deal with how we are to live with and treat each other properly. Christians and Jews believe it is no accident that God's rules for human living in a less than perfect society are to be found echoed in every society and culture. For them, it reinforces their view that God knows what is best for humanity, and that it is only by following his universal rules and standards that human beings can and will flourish.

It is obvious that these absolute and universal rules do come in very different shapes and guises, but that must not mislead us as to the underlying unity and similarity. If we reconsider the different treatment of the elderly in different parts of the world, with some being eaten and others put into old folks' homes, the apparent differences conceal one common value. It is that we should do the best we can for our old folks according to how we understand what is best. Thus the universal norm of caring for one's parents is revealed as universal, but hidden by different cultural expressions.

Some may complain that there are still societies where the elderly are left to die in the bush or on an ice-floe, because the tribe cannot afford to feed or care for them properly. So-called civilized nations are no different, however, for many of us are only too glad to get rid of elderly relatives by dumping them in old folks' homes to make others care for them.

What is interesting is that we regard such treatment of the elderly as requiring justification. It is not what we expect, or how we think people should act towards older folk. Thus we expect some kind of justification, and both groups would offer some attempt at such a justification. The need for such a justification shows that that kind of treatment is not universally accepted or expected, but is rather a departure from the usual universal norm.

If we were to ask the tribal groups to justify their treatment of the old, we would find that it was not seen as based on moral grounds but because of economic necessity. Necessity has led to the practice. If conditions were different, the elderly would be cared for properly. This makes it clear that the principle of care is not denied, but has to be set in a total context.

Similarly, there may be some who are quite happy to get rid of elderly relatives into residential care, but most of us are very uneasy about having to take such a step. Families often struggle and keep on struggling till only the threat of a breakdown drives them to look for help in caring for elderly dependent relatives. Most of us are clearly critical of those who live as if they have no responsibility for the elderly. There is a universal norm, which, like all norms, may conflict with and be set alongside other norms and requirements. That it is sometimes overridden does not change its status as a norm.

Much of the emphasis on the so-called diversity across cultural boundaries in fact arises from a misunderstanding of the actual meaning and significance of things within their cultural setting and a lack of imagination in seeing how different expressions may still express exactly the same principle within an appropriate cultural context.

Relativism runs into problems, too, when we examine the apparent diversity of moral standards in detail, and discover that instead of endless variation we have variation on a set of clearly defined themes. These themes are universal and point to absolute values and principles, even if they retain different cultural aspects.

The relativist cheat

The relativist is making a subtle move which is illegitimate. He claims to be offering us an accurate description of the way things are in the world. He appears to be describing the state of affairs in matters of morality and trying to tell it like it is. Unfortunately, somewhere along the line, he moves from describing how things are to telling us what to do about it. He moves from telling us that there is an endless variety in morality, and that there are no absolute and universal standards, to the view that we need to be tolerant with each other to cope with that moral diversity. He moves from a *de*scription to a *pre*scription. He moves from telling us that we have a problem in morality to offering to cure the disease and remove the problem. Relativism is the disease and tolerance is the cure.

We have argued that the relativist case is faulty on two entirely different grounds. But let us, for the moment, allow the relativist to have his case. Let us accept that he is quite right when he says that morality varies and there are no universal moral standards. The proof for this is in no way a proof for quite a different point all together. That is the point that tolerance is the only possible and correct response to the situation of relativism. There are two different arguments at work here. The first is that the relativist needs to provide us with two separate and different arguments for the two different points he is trying to make. He does argue for moral diversity, but he does not offer evidence to support the value of tolerance as the only and best cure.

The second argument is that even if he were to offer just such an argument, he would be uncomfortably hoist with his own petard. If it is in fact true that moral diversity rules and that there are no absolute universal standards, it seems like a logical fallacy to suggest that there is one universal and absolute cure for this disease, and that is that at all times and in all places every one of us should be tolerant. Tolerance, on this view, becomes exactly the universal value and standard which the relativist denies can or does exist.

The relativist cheats, then, in two ways. He moves illegitimately from a description to a prescription without support and argument. He then makes his cure and prescription a universal and absolute cure for a relativist disease, which, if it were true, would inevitably rule out the very cure itself.

The limits of tolerance

We live in a society where tolerance is proclaimed as one of the great virtues. 'Live and let live' is a motto for many of us in practice, if not so much in theory. We believe in the benefits of being tolerant and accepting. But how far does this go and how far ought it to go? Imagine that you are walking along a street on a fine day in your home town. God is in his heaven and all is right with the world. You are happy and tolerant. Suddenly a crazed person grabs you by the lapels and stares unseeingly into your eyes. He screams a question into your face. 'Have you seen any tolerant people lately?'

You are just about to break the good news that you are, in fact, tolerance personified, when he says something else. 'I hate tolerant people. Whenever I find a tolerant person, I kill him.'

At this point it may well be that you are faced with a little problem. Do you confess to being tolerant or not?

The example is designed to show that, while we may embrace tolerance as a positive value in society, it soon runs into difficulties. This is not simply from crazed tolerance-killing individuals, but from anyone and everyone whose views, beliefs, attitudes and actions are unacceptable to the majority of society and may even pose a fundamental threat to the very existence and freedom of that society.

What are the limits of tolerance? For tolerance must have some kind of limit. How far can we tolerate intolerance? Are we prepared to tolerate people who wish to molest children, undermine democracy, use violence against the defenceless, and threaten the existence and well-being of society itself? Tolerance cannot but be intolerant of intolerance. How far can and ought we to tolerate intolerance? It almost goes without saying that this is especially difficult in the case of tolerance itself. How far can we tolerate intolerance of tolerance?

These arguments are designed to show that the so-called virtue of tolerance is not quite the cure-all it seems to be proclaimed to be. Morally speaking, the limits of tolerance are crucial to the survival and well-being of society. These very limits will enshrine the key values of a society and offer a much broader, but infinitely more secure, basis of morality than tolerance alone.

Relativism relativized

This chapter suggests that one of the apparently major approaches to morality in our culture, and one of the main challenges to traditional morality, is seriously and fatally flawed. In its statement and in its support, in its application and in its solution, relativism fails to make sense on its own terms, in the light of the evidence, and in terms of what it offers as a substitute for the moral standards and outlooks which traditional morality has offered. Both its claims – to have discovered a disease and a cure for that disease – are faulty. We must look elsewhere for a sound basis for morality.

But we must also recognize that behind the flawed relativist case is a crucial insight. Moral rules, absolutes and universals must have particular applications. Morality has to be applied if it is to be of any use at all. This is the challenge to all moralities. It is not so much whether or not their principles and rules are worthy and laudable, but how they actually work in practice. Rules and principles need to be applied into living situations. An adequate morality will work not merely at a theoretical level. It will also be genuinely applicable in the practical settings and for the real dilemmas posed by our everyday situations and issues.

Chapter *five*

Gallons *into pint pots*

*O*ur family doesn't usually buy the *Radio Times* with its weekly outline of radio and television programmes. But there are exceptions to that rule. When I know that my name will be in the pages I love to see it down in black and white. I had been invited to take part in a Radio One programme with Annie Nightingale and was pretty excited about the programme and about meeting the well-known disc-jockey. The programme was called *Mailbag*, and it was to be a discussion on the idea that Christianity was eyewash. I bought the *Radio Times* on the correct day. There was a list of those taking part in the programme and my name was there. It read: 'Dr David Cook – a professional Christian.' I thought it sounded a bit odd to be called a professional Christian, but recognized that that was better than being called an amateur one.

The programme was live, and despite all my attempts to find out what we were going to discuss in any detail, the reply was always, 'Let's just play it by ear. Spontaneity is the key.' All I could discover was that during the programme, Annie would play some tapes and then ask me to comment. They still refused to tell me what was on the tapes. This seemed to be taking spontaneity a bit far and more likely to produce total silence than riveting broadcasting.

The programme got under way and seemed to be going fine, until they came to the first tape. It was a recording of the Hindenburg disaster, when a dirigible or balloon designed to carry passengers exploded into flames. The passengers were literally burning to death, and all the while the radio commentator was hysterically describing the terrible tragedy. The tape ended and Annie asked me to explain to the waiting British public why God had allowed this to happen.

The problem of suffering is a very complicated and difficult one which requires slightly more time and attention than can be managed in three or four minutes in the midst of a record and chat show. But the nature of broadcasting is always in danger of seeking simplistic accounts of complex issues. This was brought home to me when I listened to a member of the Stock Exchange giving a three-minute interview about the 'Big Bang' or computerization of the Stock Exchange. It had taken two years to organize and implement this change. It will take many years to get the whole system functioning properly; yet in three minutes this man was expected to explain the whole thing to the listeners. He was being asked to give a simplistic solution to a very complicated question and issue.

This seems increasingly the case at many levels of life. The media may well trivialize issues and questions by compressing the treatment of questions into the broadcasting time available, rather than into the time necessary to answer and deal with the matter thoroughly. The same trend happens in the college and university world, where students are constantly begging to be told the one book to read in order to understand an issue, or the simple guide to all they need to know on any topic. Like the rest of us, they are looking for simplistic answers to complicated questions.

It is important to see that this is not the same as looking for simple and straightforward answers which may well be proper and complete answers. Rather it is an attempt to find a shortcut. It is a way of avoiding hard work and hard thinking. It is a means of refusing to face up to the real difficulties in things. It stems from a desire to have a neat package, even if not everything is dealt with properly. In the end it is a kind of laziness on our part. The problem is that the so-called expert easily falls into the trap of reinforcing this attitude. The teacher may enjoy being seen as a guru and guide on every issue and be happy to proffer simplistic solutions to very complex questions.

A colleague whose work in the AIDS field has made him a recognized authority recently complained at the way a little experience is taken as sufficient basis for the most sweeping of judgments. We like the sound of our own voices and the feeling of importance we gain from being called upon as an 'expert'. Inevitably, we will end up in giving simplistic answers, if we understand neither the issues involved nor the proper ways of dealing with those questions.

In matters of morality, we find this same trend. When people are confronted with an ethical issue and begin to think seriously about it, they very soon realize that it is more complicated than they imagined. If we try to understand the issue of abortion and its morality, for instance, we will find that not only do people have different views, but that there are many different aspects to the problem. Working through these takes time and effort. Given a situation of brutal rape where a pregnancy results for a fifteen-year-old, the question of whether or not an abortion is morally permissible will raise difficult issues. There are complicated questions involved, of crime and punishment, rape and its impact, life and its sanctity, medical and psychological care and treatment, and long-term results whatever happens.

While many of us may be quite clear about what we feel is right or wrong in such a situation, it is obvious that our society is made up of people who would give very different answers to the question, and who would emphasize different aspects and principles in any discussion. We may be tempted to try to shortcut such discussions and plump for just one feature. Of course, it will be the feature we think is the most important one. But that would be to ignore the wider dimensions of the problem. The danger is of giving a simplistic answer to a complex question.

This kind of approach, of giving simplistic answers to complicated questions, is called *reductionism*. Reductionism is the move to reduce an issue or question to one aspect or theme which, it is claimed, will solve the problem. Unfortunately, it reduces it only by leaving out what is vital and crucial to understanding and necessary for a proper response to the issue involved. Some examples may help us grasp how the reductionist actually operates.

The Marxist reduction

When the strict Marxist is questioned on an issue, or is trying to give an account of it, he or she suggests that everything can and must be understood in purely economic terms. Everything can be reduced without remainder to some account of economic functioning within a society. The pure Marxist believes that the way to understand a culture, the roles of people within that culture, and even the historical process itself is in terms of economics. The Marxist thus describes whatever happens, as the result of economic roles and functioning. This may be one reason why there is often such a problem over human rights and what significance they are to have in a society. If you believe that an economic explanation is sufficient for everything, talk of human rights is not some absolute claim, but rather the product of certain kinds of economic functions. Thus art, morality, education, literature, music and social norms are all reducible to economic explanation.

If a Marxist were to try to explain the rise of feminism in the latter part of the twentieth century, he or she would look particularly at the way in which economic factors have played a key role. The World Wars led to the use of women in factories to replace the men who were off fighting elsewhere. With that change of role for women came spending power and earning power for them. This meant that women were now free to spend money on themselves and to have their desires fulfilled.

This change in economic status led to a change in social behaviour and an increasing demand by women to be taken seriously in the economic settings in which they worked. Women claimed that they should be treated as individuals in their own right and not merely as appendages of men. This led to a demand for equality for women both of treatment and of opportunity. This emphasis led in turn to women going out and about more and to changed attitudes towards home, housework and marriage. Thus the great sexual revolution and changes of role for both men and women in our society have not arisen because of technology, the discovery and development of the pill, or some ideal philosophy of justice and fairness. It can be explained without remainder by the changing economic climate and roles.

There are two things we need to note about this kind of explanation. The first is that it contains more than a grain of truth. One of the twisted things that happens because of fear of Marxism and Communism is that we can fail to see what is accurate and correct in the Marxist analysis. Economic changes do matter. They have played a vital role in the changing status of women. But that must not blind us to the fact that the Marxist is mistaken in making part of the truth into the whole of the truth. The Marxist is correct in affirming the importance of economic roles and functioning, but wrong in denying that anything else matters.

The second thing we need to note is that the pure Marxist reduces everything to economic terms without a remainder. The problem here lies in the reduction. For there are other factors and forces that need to be taken into consideration if we are to understand properly what is happening. It is hard to see that technology, new medical advances, concern for justice and fairness and exposure to a wider and more varied world can all be reduced to economic terms with no remainder at all. To grasp a situation or a social movement in all its complexity requires an analysis of every kind of social, economic, cultural and moral force and factor, rather than simply focusing on one of these terms.

The Marxist offers an account which is not so much simple as simplistic. Its simplistic nature arises from its failure to do justice to other crucial features in a society or situation. Understanding these features is necessary if we are to grasp fully what is happening and give an adequate account of what has happened.

The biological reduction

In vitro fertilization, artificial insemination, surrogate motherhood, genetic engineering and the continuing debate over abortion have raised the issue of when life begins. The wide variety of responses to this question have concentrated on looking at the biological evidence to see when life begins. For some, it is perfectly obvious that life must begin at the moment of fertilization when the egg and the sperm are united. For others, life only properly begins at the moment of implantation when the fertilized egg fastens on to the wall of the womb. For others, life seems to begin when a woman first feels the baby moving within her womb (called quickening). For others it is when the baby could survive outside the womb, supported by all the modern care systems which high technology medicine can offer. This would set viability as the criterion of when life begins. For others, it makes sense to talk of life beginning only when the fetus has gone its full term and is born. Some argue that life begins only when genuine and totally independent existence is possible. On this basis some of us have not reached that stage of life even at forty or fifty.

A strict biological view seeks to resolve the question of when life begins purely in biological terms. The problem is that it then attempts to explain every aspect of life by moving the analysis back to the basic biological data. We are as we are because of our genetic make-up. We do what we do because of our biological heredity. Humanity and its behaviour are thus to be understood as fully explicable in purely biological terms. Conflict, love, relationships and their breakdown are all explicable in solely biological ways.

Like the Marxist, those who offer a strictly biological account of humanity and society have fastened on a crucial aspect of human being and life. We cannot and must not deny that biology plays a key role in who and what we are and what we do. But the partial explanation does not explain the whole. There is a reductionism at work here which reduces everything to biological functioning without remainder. Life is not like that and humanity is not simply that. The simple explanation has fallen into the trap of becoming a simplistic reductionism.

This may be illustrated by the fact that even if we could reach agreement about a biological definition of when life begins, that would not tell us what value to place on that life and on the other stages in the life process. Biology does not carry within it a simple or clear moral value. Some will argue that evolutionary theory does contain such a value based on the survival of the fittest. Our very reaction to that notion, and our concern for those who are sick, unfit, and, in biological terms, 'not worth keeping alive', reveal that morality is far more than the survival of the fittest. If the critic complains that the biological development of the notion of survival of the fittest now contains care for the sick and vulnerable, it is no longer clear what is meant by survival of the fittest. It now seems that everything is included in it and nothing excluded.

Here the Marxist too can come to our aid. In drawing attention to the key role of economic factors, the Marxist reminds us of the complexity of humanity and society. For a full and complete account of human nature, we need economic, social, cultural, moral and spiritual descriptions as well as biological ones. The biological reduction is inadequate.

The Freudian reduction

There are many more reductionist moves and philosophies on offer in our society, and the very variety should alert us to the inadequacy of any one reductionist account. Some are much more significant and have had a much greater impact than others, and the Freudian account is such a one.

Freud suggested that it was possible to understand human behaviour by reference to two key principles. These were sexuality and aggression. Our relationships centre around these two themes, and all our personal struggles and our relationship difficulties arise from the ways we come to terms (or fail to come to terms) with these moving forces in our psychical make-up.

Of course, there are now a wide variety of Freudians, but the central thrust of his approach is to reduce all our human problems to issues of sexuality and aggression. By examining the id, the ego and the super-ego, and by recounting clinical cases with his explorations and discoveries, he offers very detailed accounts of the development of human sexuality and of how we cope with our aggressive instincts.

This is not the place for a detailed critique of Freud, though his use of the abnormal as a guide for normality must raise hard questions for the validity of his approach. It is enough to realize that Freud is again offering a reductionist account which claims that all that is crucial about being human can be understood through the filter of Freudian analysis and categories. In making this comprehensive claim, the importance and significance of everything else is squeezed out. The reductionist approach takes one important fact about human beings and makes it function as the sole explanation for everything. The Freudian reduction is inadequate, for it fails to do justice to the complexity of human beings and their relationship patterns in terms of their economic, social, cultural, moral and spiritual aspects.

Procrustes revisited

Procrustes was an ancient Greek who loved to have visitors. He was such a hospitable person that whenever anyone went to stay with him, he insisted that they stay overnight. He had a comfortable guest bedroom. The only negative thing about Procrustes was that he was a perfectionist. He liked things to be exact. When he invited a guest to occupy his guest bed, he meant just that. Occupation of the *whole* of the guest bed. If the bed was exactly six feet long, then Procrustes wanted every foot of the bed to be occupied. If I had gone to see Procrustes, I would have been a disappointment to him. I am only five feet seven inches tall. There would be more of the bed than there is of me. But torture racks are wonderful things. A lengthy stretch on the rack would soon ensure that Procrustes was satisfied and that I, in my new elongated state, occupied the bed completely.

I once had a student from Nigeria. He was six feet seven inches in height. He would have been a big disappointment to Procrustes, for there would have been more of him than there was of the bed. But axes are wonderful things. With a little chopping here and there, lopping off feet and part of the head, the student would have fitted the bed perfectly and Procrustes again would have been a happy man.

Procrustes, in this silly example, behaves exactly as the reductionist behaves. The reductionist, whether Marxist, Freudian or biological, comes along with his or her Procrustean bed or framework of thinking. If the data do not fit in with the theory, the facts are stretched in order to make them fit the philosophy. If, on the other hand, there are still facts left over which do not fit neatly into the framework of thought, these facts are chopped off all together and ignored.

Beware the reductionist who offers us simplistic moral solutions to very complicated moral dilemmas and issues. The price we have to pay for the reduction is that facts are either stretched to ensure a snug fit with the theory or they are ignored to try to leave the theory intact. Genuine explanations and solutions must be able to respond to and deal with all the facts, however uncomfortable for the theory in question. Reductionist accounts are inadequate as total explanations of morality.

Before we leave this chapter, a thought may have occurred to the reader. It is that what you have been reading itself falls into the trap you have been reading about: I have given (some might claim) a reductionist account of the various philosophies of Marx, Freud and biological ethics. To that charge I plead guilty, but offer in my defence a test. What have I omitted that is unfair to each view or that would save it from my critique? In what ways have I stretched the accounts or the facts in order to make my point in a way that is unfair or that cheats?

Rather, what I have tried to offer is a simple yet realistic account of these views of morality and some important criticisms. Simplicity is not the same as being simplistic or reductionistic. But what this does show is that it is not easy to avoid reductionism in all its forms, so we need to be on our guard, checking the facts and the genuine comprehensiveness of any account we are given. An adequate morality will have to deal with the whole of our human existence and be relevant to all that we are and do.

Chapter *six*

Do-it-yourself *morality*

*I*t was a sultry day in Washington DC and I had been invited to cool off at a poolside in the suburbs. It was very pleasant indeed, except for the outrageous behaviour of two small boys. They were noisy and troublesome, and kept jumping on people. Exasperated, I took it upon myself to have a friendly word, suggesting that there were other ways of behaving which would add to the pleasure of all of us. One of the boys looked me straight in the eye and said, 'Mister, I am my own boss.' He sums up the philosophy of so many of us. We are our own bosses.

This approach to morality was brought home to me when I was at school. Every now and then the behaviour of the pupils became too much for the teaching staff. They would unfurl a banner across the main staircase. It read, 'Manners maketh man.' Our headmaster stopped me one day and asked what I thought about the slogan. Being a generally obnoxious child, I suggested that it ought to read, 'Man maketh manners.' He was not amused. But, unknown to me, I was actually articulating a common approach to morality. It suggests that morality is purely a human creation, and its roots are found in the philosophy of *existentialism*.

Morality and choice

At the heart of existentialism is an emphasis on the individual. This arises from the existentialist analysis of life which stresses that the world and human beings are pointless and meaningless. The existentialist believes that there is no meaning in any one thing and there is no meaning in everything as a whole. He particularly concentrates on the features of life which are hard to understand. Suffering, death and chaos are the themes which lie at the very centre of existentialist writing in novels and drama. Indirectly, the existentialist is trying to express in a meaningful way that everything is meaningless. There is no point to anything or to everything.

The existentialist believes that the only way to cope with this kind of meaninglessness is to create our own meaning. This is done by stressing the importance of the individual and of choice. Each individual creates meaning and purpose by the choices he or she makes.

Søren Kierkegaard, the nineteenth-century Danish philosopher, argued that the crowd is a lie. By that he seems to mean that when we are part of a crowd we behave in ways in which we would never behave if we were on our own. In a crowd we hide behind other people and allow ourselves to be carried along by them. We say and do things which are not authentic to our own personal beliefs and attitudes, as long as we are simply one of the crowd. The only cure for this is to live an authentic life. That means each one of us has to take full responsibility for his or her own self. We must face up to life and every situation by ourselves and for ourselves. This is the only authentic way to live. We are shaped by our past, yet open to the future. So we must act in the present by committing ourselves to a way of life which is genuinely our own and no-one else's. In the light of what I am, what has happened to me and what I can be, I make myself and my future by the choices I make.

This inevitably emphasizes the importance of personal choice. The existentialist is extremely scathing about the fruitfulness of depending on reason or emotion. Neither gives us an accurate picture of reality or helps us cope with life as it really is, so we must *not* rely on logical thought or our romantic feelings. Reason only helps us understand what we know already. It doesn't take us anywhere at all, as we can see from looking at rational argument. In the conclusion, you get only what is already implicit in the premises. Reason takes us nowhere.

The realm of feeling and emotion is of no more help. It tries to escape from the harsh realities of life. Romanticism is the outcome of this refusal to cope with and accept reality. Emotion retreats from the harshness of the here and now. But it is a lie and unauthentic.

To be a human being means to exercise our wills. Willing is the essence of human being. What it means to be truly and fully human is to be able to make choices for ourselves. This is what separates us from the rest of reality. Things are simply there at hand for us to manipulate as we choose. We, on the other hand, are self-conscious, willing agents, who are able to make choices and to act in the light of those choices. We have self-awareness and can direct ourselves to particular ends. This is what authentic living is all about. It is about making choices.

We need to recall that the existentialist is also stressing the futility and pointlessness of everything, so he must be careful here not to fall into the trap of self-contradiction. He seeks to avoid this by making the point that it is because of the very fact of the meaninglessness of everything that the only thing left to human beings, as a mark of protest and a glorious but vain attempt to create meaning, is to make a choice. This is the very essence of humanity. It is to face up to the pointlessness of everything by creating meaning where there is none. That creation of meaning happens in and through the choices we make. It does not matter, therefore, what choices we make, as long as we do make choices. It does not matter *what* we choose. It only matters that we choose.

This does not imply that choice is like sticking a pin in a list of names in a book to choose a name for a new baby. To choose properly is to will and then to support that act of will by ensuring that the rest of our life and being is offered to carry out what was willed. Choice implies commitment. Choosing is the commitment of the whole of our being to the execution of our choices in the world in which we live.

One of the clearest examples of such choosing is found in the pages of Jean-Paul Sartre. He tells the story of a young

Frenchman during the Second World War. His father was a traitor to the Free French and betrayed his nation to the Germans as a *collaborateur*. The young man and his brother longed to atone for their father's treachery. The older brother had gone off to fight for the Free French and had been killed. This left the mother of the family totally dependent on her younger son for the physical necessities of life as well as for psychological help and solace. Nevertheless, the young man burned to go and avenge his brother's death, to make up for his father's betrayal and to fight for the freedom of the nation he loved. This meant having to leave home and going to England to join the French Resistance there. The choice was plain, but what was he to do?

Sartre stresses that it is in fact an impossible choice. This is not unusual, for so are all the choices we have to make. The world is a disordered, random place and there is no meaning to be found in events or in history. The young man had to make a choice. The only failure on his part would be to fail to make a choice. Although, in a perverse sort of way, that would in reality be a kind of choice, it would still be unauthentic. The authentic choice is to take either of the two options. It does not really matter which one he chooses. What does matter is that in making the choice, the young man commits himself totally and utterly to carrying through that choice and to trying to make it a reality.

The existentialist approach to morality stresses that choice is the fundamental factor in being moral. Morality lies not in what is chosen, but in the very act of making the choice and in the commitment to fulfilling what is intended by that choice.

This comes down to the view that we make morality by our choices. Each and every one of us must decide for ourselves. We create moral standards. We decide what we shall live by and what is right and wrong as far as we are concerned. The traditional picture of the rebellious teenager who, in growing up, revolts against the values and standards of society and of his parents is typical of us all. The person who then emerges as an adult, on this view, is someone who decides issues for himself or herself and refuses to accept the authority of anyone else. We are to be our own bosses.

When the philosophers in Oxford heard of this philosophy and read what was being suggested, their response was typical of philosophers. On the one hand, they realized that the existentialist had put his finger on an important feature of morality. The will is crucial, and deciding as an individual is part of what responsibility, autonomy and freedom require. On the other hand, the Oxford dons thought that, like most continental philosophy, it had all been taken too far. After all, if we all did whatever we wanted and decided to do, society would collapse. It was unreasonable, and not a sensible way to organize a morality.

Morality and prescriptions

Thus they developed the philosophy of *prescriptivism*, which is actually a variation on quite a different continental philosophy based on the work of Immanuel Kant. It was agreed that morality was centred on the individual's making choices. But in the process of choosing, it was vital to choose only what everyone else in the same situation would also choose. This was called the *principle of universalizability*. Each of our decisions must be universalizable to prevent us from cheating and begging the question in our own favour. We have to ask what other people would do in the same situation, and do that, unless there is some overriding factor which allows us to do something else. Such an overriding factor would then mean that everyone else would do the same as we actually did, once they realized the importance of the overriding factor.

This approach to morality preserves the emphasis on individual responsibility and the importance of choice, but puts it in the context of what is rational and logical. Morality must be reasonable, and that means it has to be what all reasonable people would do in the same circumstances.

Prescriptivism and existentialism both place the focus of

morality firmly on the choices made by human beings either as individuals, or as individuals representing every other individual. Thus morality is a human creation. It is human beings who decide what counts as morality, and they define the nature and content of that morality. In that sense, anything and everything can be seen as a moral issue if we choose to make it so. We decide what the content of morality is. Today it might be about how we treat each other, and tomorrow it might be about being careful not to step on paving stones.

It is crucial to see that both these approaches to morality take the form of prescribing what should be done in a situation. For the existentialist, making a moral decision is like writing a prescription telling oneself what to do. For the prescriptivist, making moral decisions is like writing a prescription, not only for oneself, but for everyone else in the world who faces the same problem and issues. All that is then required to be moral is to follow the advice in the prescription.

Meaning in meaninglessness

There is a way to undermine the existentialist's whole attempt to make choice the central feature of morality. It is to draw attention to the inability of existentialist philosophy to get off the ground at all. If I say that everything is meaningless, the question must arise as to whether or not my statement that everything is meaningless is a meaningful or a meaningless statement. If it is a meaningful statement, then inevitably it is not true that everything is meaningless. For we have discovered one meaningful thing, *i.e.* that everything is meaningless. If, on the other hand, to say that everything is meaningless is to make a meaningless statement, then we cannot hope to understand what is being said by the existentialist. It is nonsense and meaningless.

If this argument does reduce the existentialist view to nonsense, it is not possible for the existentialist to state or argue for his philosophy without falling into contradiction. It would thus pose no threat at all to our normal understanding of morality. But we need to face up to the heart of the existentialist view in a much more rigorous way.

Tradition

In the film *Fiddler on the Roof*, the main character, a good Jewish father, finds that his daughter wants to marry a Gentile. He cries out in song. The theme of the song is tradition, lamenting that his daughter threatens tradition not only by wanting to marry a non-Jew but also by failing to go through the usual matchmaking channels. The effrontery of young people who decide by themselves to get married without letting their families make the first moves, and plan and agree the match, threatens his tradition and the values enshrined in that tradition.

What this reveals is a strong understanding of the force of tradition and the way that the past shapes and affects us. It is odd that the existentialist usually draws our attention to the way that the past does shape and mould us, but then fails to carry through the implications of what is being propounded. The problem with the existentialist account of making choices is that it offers a picture of human beings entering into the world like a writer facing a blank page in his typewriter. It looks as if we can write anything we like. While that may be true of the writer, it is not an accurate account of being human. We enter into a world which is already shaped and moulded. We have to learn what choice means in that world, and our understanding of choice, the options in choosing, the way to choose and the results of making choices are all learned activities. In fact, society, our parents and the world in which we live shape what and how we choose much more than we often realize.

When my wife and I talked with some parents who were concerned that their children stayed up too late at nights even though they were quite young, we advised them to try an old and trusted ploy. The parents would say to their children, 'Would you rather go to bed in ten minutes or half an hour?' Naturally the children would choose to go to bed in half an hour, which in fact was the time the parents had decided on in the first place. What looks like giving a choice is really a way of setting limits on what can be chosen.

The classic example of this tactic is the question, 'Have you stopped beating your wife yet? Answer "Yes" or "No".' The question looks like an open one, but, in fact, it limits the answers and implies either that you were a wife-beater and have stopped or that you still are a wife-beater. It also implies that you have a wife and are violent. The only way to cope with the question is to refuse to accept its categories at all.

The world around us already has set forms, traditions and means of understanding and expressing reality. We learn this and have to acquire the categories necessary in order to function properly in our world. We are not given blank pages with the possibility of interpreting the world in any way we like. We are *taught* how to view the world, express its nature and communicate with others in order to make relationships at all. Our tradition shapes us, and all too often we do not even notice that it has happened.

In teaching in a university context, one aim of mine is to try to help my students to think better than I do. The problem is that often I have to teach them how to think and how to develop their thinking. In teaching them to do that, I may also be limiting their thinking to the ways in which I am able to think and able to teach others to think. It is very hard indeed to break away from taught, learned and in-built structures. Even in order to question those structures, as the existentialist seeks to do, we are required to use the tools learned by those structures.

The existentialist account of being human fails to deal fully and adequately with the way our tradition shapes and moulds us morally. We imbibe our values from our homes, families, educational systems, friends, and the world around us. Our morality is not purely individual. It is part of a community and tradition in which we live and function.

The Old and New Testaments clearly understand this. The moral rules and standards of life are not just matters for the individual. They are for every individual as a member of the community. The moral commands are given for all to follow as individuals and as part of the community. When one acts, others are affected. When one suffers, all can suffer. The pictures of the church as a body or as a building (1 Corinthians 12:12–27; 1 Peter 2:4–5) stress that fine balance between being both individuals and members of the community. We are both, and morality is clearly about both.

Being and choosing

The existentialist picture of what it means to be a person and to make choices is faulty and inadequate. It begins by separating different aspects of being human. Reason and emotion are rejected in favour of the will. Like the reductionist, the existentialist is correct in what he affirms and wrong in what he denies. It is obviously the case that the will plays a key role in moral decision-making. It is not at all clear that reason and feeling are irrelevant in that process. If we are to make an informed choice rather than a guess, we need to know the facts of the situation. We need to know what has happened and what will happen. We need to reflect on the options available to us and what they entail. We need to understand the nature of what we are going to do and what it actually involves. We need to know what the likely consequences are and what are the likely probabilities in the situation. All of these require the use of reason. Thinking and understanding are fundamental to informed and sensible moral decision-making.

It is likewise foolish to underestimate the role of our feelings and emotions in morality. Morals and ethical issues affect us deeply, and it is no surprise that our feelings are intimately involved. When we hear about atrocities and man's inhumanity to man, we are moved by what we see and hear. It is part of our human nature to be affected and to be able to respond to others and enter imaginatively and sympathetically into their predicaments.

I once spoke at a medical conference, along with a paediatrician who was involved with severely handicapped children. As he spoke of the work he did to preserve their life and to improve the quality of that life, the students complained that he was emotionally involved. He responded by asking, 'If you were seriously ill, would you rather have a doctor who felt nothing at all about your suffering, or one who was deeply involved?' He stressed that it was not a matter of technical skill or its application. It was a matter of the manner and motive in and behind the use of those skills. The human beings we value and seek to emulate are those who are concerned and emotionally involved with others. The cold fish who is stand-offish and refuses to make warm and responsive relationships is very far from our ideal picture of a human being.

It is thus clear that the existentialist account of choice and the underlying notion of being are not accurate. Choice is inevitably wrapped up in an amalgam of thinking and reflection, as well as feeling and emotion. To isolate one from the others all together is a failure to appreciate the complexity of human nature and of human choice.

The prescriptive prescription

The prescriptivist tries to save the existentialist insight from this critique by stressing the role of reason in moral decision-making. The principle of universalizability is designed to achieve that end. The problem is that universalizing does not add anything at all to the morality or immorality of an action. It does tell us that consistency matters, but it leaves the door open to regarding as moral any and every kind of thing, theme, action and response. It seems clear that not everything can be classed as an item for morality. To arrange flowers, to evaluate art, to respond to music are all aesthetic responses, but this is not morality. Even less near the mark is the idea that we could choose to make any trivial action such as 'touching wood' a moral requirement, and react with moral condemnation when people failed to do so. Such an action might be a feature of a culture or of superstition, but this is clearly distinguishable from morality. The content of morality is not a totally open matter. Not all behaviour or all things can be appropriately counted as morally significant.

By concentrating on the *process* of reflecting on morality, there is a failure to think through the importance of the *content* of morality. It is not true that human beings make morality. The existence of moral codes at the heart of religion and the role of revelation point in the direction of a morality which stems not from human thought and will, but from a divine perspective.

Obviously, not all are convinced of the reality of the divine will and command in moral terms, though it would be interesting to ask whether human beings, left to their own devices, would have opted for monogamy rather than polyandry and polygamy. But the natural world and the nature of being human seem to point in the direction of natural laws which have a moral basis.

Even if there are problems over defining what is natural, this does not change the general fact that the way that the world operates and the ways in which human beings function point to certain courses of action which are good for people and to others which are bad. There is a morality in the nature of things which means that certain kinds of actions and behaviour lead to certain bad results and other kinds of action and behaviour lead to good results. We know intuitively and instinctively (perhaps more than we like to admit) that the good is to be pursued and the evil to be avoided. We do not make this up, but rather discover this moral dimension in the world around us and in other people. It is neither an individual nor a communal choice. It confronts human beings and demands an appropriate moral response from them.

In the same way, the presence of universal moral norms seems hard to ignore, taking mere prescription as the basis for morality.

At the very least, human beings must be remarkably similar, with similar concerns, to have ended up with such universal agreement over basic morality. It seems to reveal something about human nature itself which is more than simply choosing.

While human choice, both individual and corporate, is important in morality, and especially in understanding what it means to be responsible, free men and women, morality is much more than just the single factor of human choice. Morality is never a do-it-yourself matter, and is not only a do-it-together activity.

Chapter *seven*

What *you feel is right*

*O*ne feature of moral debate that many people find distressing is that people get excited, angry and bitter when they disagree over moral issues. When the pro-life groups wish to gain support for their strong moral stance on abortion, for example, they send postcards that show pictures of eighteen-week fetuses sucking their thumbs. They draw attention to the fact that these fetuses could be aborted under the current British abortion law. The impact of seeing a child within the womb sucking a thumb arouses our emotions.

It is the same with peace campaigners who try to alert the world to the immorality of war according to their perspective. They display posters of children running naked down a dirt road thronged with refugees. These children are covered in napalm-burn blisters. 'War harms little children and other living things' is the kind of slogan on such posters. Our stomachs heave and the taste in our mouths is distinctly unpleasant.

Both groups realize that emotion plays a key part in our moral attitudes towards features of society. If people's feelings can be affected, they may be sufficiently moved and inspired to do something about the issue and to make a moral stand. Feelings are thus seen as the key to critical action and response.

It is not only in the realm of information and propaganda that the role of feelings is important. Language itself is a carrier of emotion. The words that we use and the way that we say things can have a very different impact and effect on our emotions. If I tell a patient that what we are going to do in her operation tomorrow is to 'evacuate the uterus', it sounds coolly clinical and objective. If, however, I tell her that we are going to 'scrape out the baby', I would expect quite a different reaction.

It is not just what we say but also the way we say it which fundamentally alters the reactions we engender. If I had to break the news to someone that a close and much-loved relative has died, I could choose the setting, prepare the ground, be sensitive to possible reactions, and ensure privacy. Or I could tell the person suddenly in the middle of a public street. The actual words I use may be the same in either case, but each option would take on quite a different feel, and the feelings about how I broke the news, both at the time and especially later, would be quite different. Our language, especially when it comes to dealing with moral issues, carries values and can arouse emotions and feeling.

Facts and feelings

This practical use of words and contexts hits an old philosophical nail on the head. It goes back to the seventeenth and eighteenth centuries when there was a great debate about what we know and how we know it. One side – the rationalists – argued that *reason* was the basis of true knowledge and the pathway to achieve certain and indubitable knowing. The other side – the empiricists – were very sceptical about the capacity of reason to take us anywhere at all. They stressed that real knowledge came through the *senses*, and that the only absolutely certain experience was what could be tested and validated by means of one of the five senses.

Those who stressed the importance of sense-experience in knowing realized that reason had some kind of part to play. They drew a distinction between two kinds of knowledge. The first was what was true by definition, like mathematics and logic. The other was what was true from sense-experience. We know it because we see, touch, taste, smell or hear it.

This distinction was very helpful in distinguishing what we know by deduction and by induction. Deductive knowledge comes from and through reason. Inductive knowledge comes only from our sensory experience of the world. Deduction and induction divide knowledge into two neat categories – what reason tells us and what sense-experience tells us.

But this does not help us know where we are to put moral, religious or aesthetic language and experience.

In the debate that raged, all kinds of solutions were presented. But those who stressed the role of sense-experience were so convinced that they were correct about reality, knowledge and meaning that they framed a principle to test whether or not something was a meaningful statement about reality. This was the famous *principle of verifiability*, which suggested that a statement had meaning if, and only if, it could be tested by sense-experience.

We shall not concern ourselves with all that followed from this, except to see that moral talk was, on this basis, literally meaningless. If I want to test the statement that 'telling lies is a wicked, evil thing for anyone to do', there is no *one* or *any* sense experience by which I can test the statement. None of my senses helps me to know if the statement is true or not. Since it cannot be tested, according to the principle of verifiability, the statement must be meaningless.

The motive and aim behind this apparently odd move was to ensure that we all knew what language was based on facts and what was not. Facts were what could be tested by sense experience. Everything else must fall into a different category. It is clear that the category of reason and deduction will not do as a home for moral language. Moral standards are not obviously true by definition, and the problem of what is right and wrong is not solved by looking up the dictionary.

Thus another setting had to be found. It arose from the insight that moral talk was not about facts at all but about *feelings*.

Emotivism

There is a theory of ethics which builds on the role of emotion in our moral language. It begins from the point that moral language is different from scientific language. Scientific language is really talk about facts and what is actually the case. Moral language is not about things which exist or factual states of affairs. Morality is about feelings and attitudes. This means that for the emotivist, ethical terms are really being used like interjections. They are just ways of saying 'Ooh!' and 'Aah!'

Technically, the emotive theory of ethics claims that all there is to our moral beliefs and convictions is an attitude towards something. Words like 'good' and 'bad' are ways of expressing to each other the attitudes we have. This implies that the meaning of ethical statements is to be found by realizing that such language expresses a particular state of mind or an attitude towards something. It may not be a simple reporting of that attitude, but it is certainly an expression of it.

This makes the function of moral language rather like giving an order or writing a prescription. The imperative and prescriptive forms of language use are really what ethical statements are doing. The emotivist is concerned with the way in which moral talk actually functions, and orders and prescriptions are the best way to understand that role. Of course, there is the recognition that when language is used like this there is also an imparting of facts and a giving of information, but that is purely accidental and has nothing to do with the main aim of using moral language. But all this is highly technical and can be expressed in a simpler way.

There are two main ideas at the heart of the emotive theory of ethics. Both focus on what we are doing when we make moral statements to each other. If I say, 'Abortion is every woman's fundamental right and is a good thing,' I am telling you what I feel about abortion. In a sense, I am really saying, 'Abortion. Hurrah!' If, on the other hand, I say, 'Abortion is a murderous evil and should be forbidden at all costs,' I am really saying, 'Abortion.

Boo!' This has led some commentators to describe the emotivist position as the 'Boo-hurrah' theory of ethics.

What this view comes down to is that moral language is all about expressing our feelings. What we are actually doing when we call things good or bad, right or wrong, is telling each other that we feel positively or negatively about these things. We are expressing our attitudes and feelings. We are revealing our emotions to each other, but use moral terms as a vehicle to carry the force of what we say.

There is something else that is happening when we use moral language. It not only expresses our feelings and attitudes. It is also used to arouse the same feelings and attitudes in other people. Our use of 'good' and 'bad', 'right' and 'wrong', is designed to elicit the *same* response in others. We are trying to make people feel as deeply and as forcefully as we ourselves feel about particular issues. To do that, we use moral language which is designed to arouse emotions, which in turn will lead to action. The way to change people's moral views is not so much by arguing about facts, but rather by affecting what they feel about something. If we can arouse their feelings, they will identify with our attitudes and in turn express these in the same way as we do. Obviously, this implies that what makes people do things or not do things is the strength of their feelings. Deep and strong feelings lead to action.

A matter of personal taste

The emphasis on feeling rather than on facts in morality makes our ethical standpoints a mere matter of personal taste and preference. On this view, morality is a purely subjective affair. This means that morality depends on me and my personal preferences and tastes. It is a kind of prejudice that lies at the heart of morality. This explains the amount of both disagreement and bitterness which often accompany moral diversity. Different people feel differently about things, so inevitably there will be moral disagreement.

Subjectivism means that there are no objective or absolute facts to be found, discussed and evaluated in matters of morals. It is simply up to you and me and to what we happen to feel about things. Getting people to change their minds about moral issues is actually about getting them to change their feelings. Once their feelings have been affected, then we shall have brought about a moral change.

It ain't necessarily so

The subjective and emotive stress on morality falls into the same error as any and every reductionist approach to ethical issues and language. It takes one feature, which is in itself important, and then makes it the only and central feature of morality. But that is not necessarily so.

Obviously, our feelings and emotions *are* intimately involved in moral matters, for morality is about things and issues that matter deeply to us. This is very far from saying that our feelings are *all* that is involved in making moral judgments and statements. Likewise, it is necessarily the case that we are involved, as subjects making moral decisions, when we use moral language, but that does not mean that morality is just a matter of personal prejudice or purely an emotional reaction.

There is all too often a kind of cheating about the way people use the word 'subjective' about morality. It is obviously true that my moral judgments are subjective in the sense that they belong to me as a subject. But that sense is quite different from the negative sense which holds that there is no proper or adequate basis for an opinion or judgment. If I can offer good reasons for my view and others accept the validity of those reasons, then my views are not subjective.

When we looked at relativistic accounts of morality, we saw that there is in fact an objective, factual basis for morality. There is a general and universal agreement about what counts as morally significant, and even about what kinds of issues and laws are necessary for human being and flourishing. Murder and the sanctity of life, truth-telling and promise-keeping, and some kind of sexual ordering are all central, universal moral themes regardless of what we happen to feel about them (see chapter 4). These standards challenge me if I depart from them, even if I feel it is all right for me to do so.

This raises one crucial weakness in the stress on feeling as the basis of morality. Our feelings are notoriously volatile: we are affected by what we had for breakfast, when we last saw our girlfriend or boyfriend, and how much sleep we had last night. Our feelings come and go and may change with the weather and the time of the month. This does not seem to be the case with our moral attitudes and principles. We hold to them and expect each other to hold them in a consistent way. Lying is wrong and that is the end of it. We may think of exceptional cases where it may be justifiable to tell a so-called 'white lie', but even our careful description of it as 'white' proves that we do hold that telling lies is wrong.

What we happen to *feel* about lying or other moral rules is not really the point. In spite of what we feel, we will still recognize that the rules carry a moral force, even when we are doing something we know to be wrong. In fact, the essence of the moral struggle really comes home to many of us when we strongly desire to do something but know full well that we ought not to do it. That gap between what we *want* and what we *ought* to do reveals that morality and feeling are not one and the same thing.

When my sons misbehave and get themselves into trouble, I may feel very sympathetic and know that there, but for the grace of God, go I. I may feel a very deep concern about what they have done and what they are going through, but I may still have to judge and punish their actions as wrongdoing worthy of punishment. I have to do my duty as a parent, in spite of what I may feel. All of us know only too well that dilemma of the gap between what we feel and our duty. To do what is right is not the same as doing what we feel like doing.

We may go a little further to see that to make sense of morality and moral talk at all there must be some kind of agreement about what counts as a moral issue and what is morally relevant and irrelevant. We could not understand each other's views or hold any kind of moral discussion, far less have an argument, unless we all presupposed and accepted some kind of objective idea of moral argument, justification and debate, and of what counts as proper to put forward in that kind of setting. That we agree as to what is morally significant is not a matter of what we happen to feel or not to feel.

In that kind of moral discussion, we do not simply parade what we feel. But that is exactly what we should expect to happen, were we all to realize that the emotivist theory was correct. We would see through and throw away the trappings of moral language and get back to the basics of what we feel about things. But we do not do that. Rather, we give *reasons* for thinking that some things are right or wrong. We offer grounds and evidence in support of our moral judgment, in the belief that it is this kind of evidence and argument that will change people's minds and behaviour.

The emotivist has suggested that our moral language seeks to change people by expressing feelings rather than by appealing to facts. This does not seem to be the case, for when we warn someone that he or she ought not to take a certain course of action, we are often really saying, 'If you do that, it will end up in disaster and hurt you and other people.' There is a *descriptive* content in our moral language, which is not superficial, but lies at the very heart of what we are saying in using moral language. We are emphasizing what leads to human flourishing and wholeness and warning against what leads to human diminishing and belittling.

If the emotivist were correct, the use of moral language would be reduced to propaganda and conditioning. If the standard by which I judge the success or failure of moral language is its success or failure in arousing certain feelings, any kind of technique which aroused those feelings would be permissible and would fulfil the new aim of moral discourse. This would reduce moral discussion to any and every kind of emotional manipulation and psychological pressurizing. As long as I made people feel the appropriate response, it wouldn't matter how I evoked the feeling. In that sense, the end would justify the means. But it doesn't. Of course, moral discussion does include our feelings, but it also includes facts, descriptions and rational argument, justification and evidence.

When we talk about things being good and right, we are not always, or merely, prescribing or expressing an attitude. When we say, 'It is right to do this or that,' we think we are describing what is actually the case and not just offering a prescription. We are, rather, telling it as it is and drawing attention to the logic which lies behind moral judgments and views. Moral language does not simply give imperatives ('Do this') or express attitudes ('I don't feel very positively about this'). It also contains and deals with factual descriptions and accounts of moral reality. It uses a common understanding of what makes morality and what counts as moral. What we feel has a role in it all, but that is very far from being the be-all and end-all of it.

Chapter eight

An adequate morality?

*I*n our examination of the variety of possible sources and bases of morality, it may seem as if each and every one of these approaches is in a little box and has nothing whatsoever to do with any other approach. That is not the case. It is possible to look at moral issues and make ethical decisions purely in terms of each one of the approaches examined. In fact most of us use a mixture of all or at least some of them. We take a little of this and a bit of that and somehow or other arrive at our own special blend of morality.

The problem lies in how we make the blend. There may be little rhyme or reason for picking one aspect of a view and adding it to a different element from another theory. There may be little consistency or even method in our moral mix. That lack of consistency makes for problems, both because our own actions may be dissimilar in similar situations, and also because other people will not and cannot know how we have arrived at the decisions behind our actions. They will look for some pattern and coherence in our approach to things. They may find a haphazard mish-mash of bits and pieces. This will certainly fail to do justice to the view from which we have taken each bit and piece. We may also end up with a set of contradictory outlooks and principles which may lead to serious conflict when applied to some issues and problems.

We do, in fact, want to make the most of what we have, and to try to be consistent in our morality. We need some kind of basic framework of thinking or set of presuppositions which forms the basis of our moral understanding and enables us to approach moral questions and difficulties. In reality, especially in our secularized twentieth-century world, we seem to end up with very different frameworks of interpretation in matters of morality. What is required, then, is some way of judging between competing frameworks in order to distinguish which are more or less adequate.

One test which we might use is *internal consistency and coherence*. If a view is inconsistent and incoherent, it is a non-starter, for it does not even make sense on its own terms, never mind in relation to anything or everything else.

A second test would be how well the theory *corresponds to the facts* and to reality as we know it. If any one moral view gives a more accurate picture of ethical issues, human nature and the facts and factors we need to consider when we make moral decisions, it is obviously a more adequate account and much more reliable in facing up to the questions and issues of life.

There is a third test which I believe we cannot escape in the realm of morality. It is the actual *success or failure* of a moral theory and outlook. Morality is in the end about what actually works best. It must help us to make proper and sound moral decisions. It must make it easier for us to make those decisions and satisfy us that we have made the correct decisions. It should enhance our human existence and lead to proper human fulfilment and happiness.

Thus we are looking for a moral theory which does justice to all the different facets of morality and gives the most adequate account of the nature and content of morality. It must also work in practice and not simply be a theoretical account, however interesting and fascinating as an exercise of the mind. If it does not make a difference in practice, it will not be an adequate account of morality.

A sufficient morality?

In the light of the different ways in which people do make

decisions, we must ask why some emphasize one facet rather than another. Our critical analysis has often shown that people were correct in what they affirmed, but mistaken in what they denied. They had made part of morality the whole, and so had failed to do justice to the totality of morality. This gives us a clue as to what will be sufficient. Morality must be *comprehensive.*

That means that there has to be a sound basic set of moral principles, norms, standards and rules. While it may not be easy to reach agreement about the sources of these principles and guidelines, it is quite clear that we do all operate with certain assumptions. We need a point to lever the world and a framework of approach to the dilemmas which face us. That will mean looking at different claims about principles and seeing which claims are true. It will mean testing views that look at the nature of people and of the world and which present certain moral insights in the light of those understandings. It means taking a hard, critical look at what we call our conscience and the sense and awareness of right and wrong, which seems so much part and parcel of who and what we are. It means testing claims to intuit what is morally good and bad and seeing if such intuitions can be repeated and tested.

An adequate morality will not only be based on a clear set of principles, but will take the consequences of our actions very seriously indeed. Even though a morality based on consequences alone runs into fundamental problems, that must not blind us to the importance of what happens because of our moral choices. The results which will follow from different choices and actions we might take are a crucial part of working out what we ought to do. Consequences matter and we need to remember that.

This does not imply that *only* the consequences matter in the rightness and wrongness of what we do. There will still be times when we have to accept unfortunate consequences, foreseen or unforeseen, of right decisions we make.

A young African bride had come with her husband to Britain. Unknown to her, she was pregnant. Late one night she developed acute appendicitis. She was rushed to hospital and they operated.

They saved her life, but they also killed the baby. No-one wanted to kill the baby, but, in this case, they did not know about the pregnancy and could only go ahead with the operation. Even if they had known of the pregnancy, and if the only way to save the life of the mother was an operation which would inevitably kill the baby, they would have proceeded. They would have done what was right – saved the life of the mother – even though one of the consequences was bad. The way the world is means that doing what is right does not always lead to good results in the immediate situation. The consequences matter, but are not the sole deciding factor.

A comprehensive morality will recognize that human happiness, fulfilment and *shalom* (the biblical Hebrew word for all-round well-being) are important ingredients. What leads to human flourishing is to be encouraged. What causes human beings harm is to be avoided. We need to beware of too narrow a view of the content and nature of happiness and of too short-term a view of the benefits accruing from doing what is right and good. It is part of morality to be concerned about human happiness, though that again is not the sole deciding factor. It is certainly not the only or best motivation for moral behaviour. We can all too easily act selfishly for our own pleasure or to avoid pain and unpleasantness. What is right and good and ought to be done may not always be easy, pleasurable, or very satisfying.

We have argued that the relativist idea that right, wrong, goodness and badness vary from time to time, place to place, and person to person, is fatally flawed. We have seen that relativism in theory and in practice is not a tenable moral account. Yet its hold is very strong and we must not neglect what lies behind that strength. Part of this is the desire of all of us to know what to do in actual situations. General principles and moral absolutes are fine at the theoretical level. But we want help with the nitty-gritty of life. Relativism, even in our rejection of it, reminds us that an adequate morality must work. It must deal with the specific and particular, as well as with the universal and global. The problem with universal moral standards is that they tend to be vague and general. They need to be applied, and we need help to know how to apply them properly.

That help does not and cannot come from any account of morality which tries to reduce our understanding of morality to one aspect alone. We saw how the various attempts at moral reductionism each held important grains of truth, but made the fatal mistake of ignoring all other insights. Our human nature wants and needs solutions which are simple. But, unless our moral views deal with every aspect of an actual situation, we shall find that we cannot live by such views and that they are no adequate basis for moral decision-making. We need to maintain a proper balance of complexity and simplicity without falling into the trap of oversimplification.

Behind much of the stress on approaches based on principles and consequences lies an unstated dependence on reason. It is by *thinking* that we often work out what principles are involved in a situation and how to apply them, what consequences will follow from whatever we choose and decide, and what insights can be gleaned from various claims to have *the* moral truth. Reason is clearly part of our moral process, but so equally are our feelings and our wills. What and how we feel about issues and the nature, basis and process of choice must be catered for if our moral view is to be adequate to cope with every aspect of being human. Emotion and will cannot be ignored, though each, on its own, is an insufficient basis for morality.

We have seen, then, that a truly comprehensive morality will involve principles and consequences, happiness and fulfilment; it will be genuinely applicable to real problems and situations; it will be able to use insights from various moral perspectives; and it will maintain a proper balance between, and a place for, our reason, will and emotions.

There is another way to express this. When I use my morality and make a moral decision, I have certain motives which affect the morality of that decision. The decision will raise and rest on certain principles and rules, which give content to the moral dimension. In the light of the decision, I will do something or nothing. Any decision will lead to some action, or inaction, which itself has moral significance. Other people, as well as I myself, can ask whether the action, or the lack of action, is right or wrong in itself. My action or inaction will lead to certain consequences, and the morality of my decision will be affected by the morality of the consequences. Moral decision-making involves motives, principles, the nature of action, and results and consequences. A truly adequate moral view must give sufficient weight to all these aspects.

The Christian option

Western people have a Judaeo-Christian heritage. Our tradition shapes and moulds our views of right and wrong. The danger for many is to imagine that because it is part of our history and culture, it is out-of-date and untrue. Christians are convinced that a Christian morality is the correct moral view and is a genuinely sufficient morality.

The Christian view of morality begins with God. Morality is not seen as humanity's invention or idea. It is God's gift. What is good and bad, right and wrong, is defined and delineated by reference to God. This means that at the heart of the Christian approach to morality lies *revelation*. God reveals his moral standards to us. If you ask Christians where they get their basic moral principles from, they would all point, to a greater or lesser extent, to the Bible. Some might put their emphasis on a minimum from the Bible. 'Love your neighbour' might be as far as they are prepared to go. Nevertheless, it is still from the Scriptures that they derive their moral principles. Others might favour taking the whole of the Bible seriously as the source of Christian morality.

Both approaches have to recognize that the Bible is not a textbook of morality. It tells us the story of God's dealings with humanity. It teaches us what God is like and what humanity is and is meant to be. It then shows how we are to live in the light of that.

So there is a great deal about moral issues in the Bible, but they often arise in the context of a particular situation or problem, or as part of a much wider teaching programme. The morality usually comes after the teaching, so that, as a result of understanding the teaching, we can see what to do. But there are certainly clear sets of principles to be found in the Bible.

Law and nature

For many Christians, God's laws are expressed in human nature and the natural world. They provide a basic set of principles by which to live. But it is quite clear from the Bible, as well as from all our experience, that the world is unfortunately less than perfect. Christian teaching expresses this reality as the result of the Fall. The world and human beings have fallen short of what God wants for them. We are not what we ought to be, and we do not do what we ought to do. The world itself does not function perfectly. All this means that we cannot deduce a total and perfect morality simply from human nature and the laws of nature.

The giving of the Law, especially the Ten Commandments, was God's response to this situation. God gave minimal law which any and every society requires in order to survive and flourish as a society. We saw that every culture and moral community has some kind of rule and law about parent-children relationships, truth-telling, sexual ordering in society, the value and sanctity of life, and what belongs to an individual or group. The Ten Commandments put these rules in the context of a proper relationship with God. They seem to be saying that the only way to ensure that these five laws are kept properly is in a living relationship with God where he has his rightful and proper place.

Just as the ancient Israelites received God's laws which covered religious, social and ceremonial situations and occasions, so the Christian church has looked to God's Law in order to discern the fundamental principles for human life and society which it contains.

Unfortunately, it all too soon became obvious that our human capacity to obey God's Law was limited, and we pleased ourselves and did whatever was right in our own eyes. God sent the Old Testament prophets to recall his people to live as they were created and meant to live and be. Again and again, the call of the prophets was to return to the original relationship with God and to live with each other in such a way that justice and mercy were evident.

The Christian looks to the prophets, and to the books in the Bible that we call 'Wisdom literature' (Job, Proverbs, Ecclesiastes), in order to see what rules for living God has expressed in the history and life of the Old Testament Jewish nation.

Jesus and the new covenant

It seems that some lessons are only learned the hard way. The people of Israel repeatedly failed to be as God wanted them to be. They did not seem to get the messages that God was sending, and, even if they knew the principles to be lived by and adhered to, they seldom put them into practice. That is why the coming of Jesus was so crucial.

The danger is that we understand Jesus simply in terms of just another revelation of God. This is to put him on the same level as other claims to revelation. Jesus is not *just* a revelation of God. He is also the Saviour. Jesus came to show us what God is like. Jesus came to express in human terms all that we need to know about God. This is what 'incarnation' really means. God shows himself to us in and through Jesus. But in so doing, he is not just showing us what the standards are for human beings. He also helps us to live like Jesus and to be the men and women God created and intended us to be.

Jesus is God's visual aid. He lived a life which all men and women are to live, in terms of its moral quality. He is the perfect example to be followed and imitated. He offers new insight into the kind of love that God requires of us all. He creates a new community where that love is lived out, expressed, and shared with the world.

But Jesus does far more than that. He also restored humanity's proper relationship with God. He died in order to bring humanity back to God and his ways. He died to make us good. That is why following Jesus is not about *trying* to live the good life that he lived and taught. It is about becoming new men and women with Christ Jesus living in us. It is about what the evangelical jargon calls 'being saved'. By this we mean that we no longer live simply as fallen men and women, but we turn round to live as God wants by the power of Jesus.

That power of Jesus is ours through the Holy Spirit. This is what makes Christianity more than a do-it-yourself or even a do-it-together religion. It is doing it through the Spirit of Jesus. Jesus taught and lived out the principles and standards that God wants from us all. To love God, our neighbours as ourselves, one another as Christ has loved us, and our enemies, is what is required of us all. It is impossible, without the help of the Spirit of Jesus to enable us to be the kind of men and women we ought to be.

The rest of the New Testament is about how people first tried to live that kind of life. Of course, they often got it wrong, but this was not just another set of moral principles to be examined and then attempted. The principles of Jesus are given to us in the context of the promise of God's Holy Spirit to help us fulfil the perfect example Jesus gave. This is why the church down the ages has seen morality in terms of imitating Jesus. We are all to be like him. But, as we all very quickly discover, we need help to live like that.

There are principles at the heart of Christian morality, but these principles are embodied in Jesus Christ. We can use and apply these principles, for we have available the power of the Spirit of Jesus to live as we ought.

Christians and consequences

One difficulty with a morality that emphasizes principles is that it can ignore the consequences of morality. Christian morality does not fall into that trap. It is quite clear from creation, through the Law and into the teaching of Jesus that consequences do matter. If we live in certain ways, then the consequences will be disastrous. If we live as God intends, then blessing follows. Generally speaking, we shall find that good results follow naturally from doing good things and that evil results will follow from doing what is wrong. Of course, we can all think of exceptions to this general rule. But the exceptions must not blind us to the reality of how the world is and what human life does involve for us. The Bible recognizes exceptions, but even Job came to terms with his experience when the opposite of the general rule happened to him. In the end, goodness and badness lead to their own inevitable rewards. Results do matter.

That is why Christian morality is concerned about true happiness and fulfilment and makes sure that these are understood in terms of eternity rather than just the here and now. It is only in a proper relationship with God that we find our fulfilment and wholeness. Harmony in our personal being, in relationship with the world around, and with each other, is the promise for those who obey God's rules and walk in his ways.

Christian morality and absolutes

The church today is very hesitant to talk about absolutes, for it has been infiltrated by the relativism of society around us. Yet Christian morality expresses absolutes in terms of principles, consequences and wholeness. These are absolutely certain and non-negotiable. They are ideals which stand as a beacon to draw us nearer to God. These are the aims that we must have, and our task is to seek to achieve them as we grow more and more like Jesus.

Some people seem to think that this will do away with all complexity, but that is to fail to understand the nature of absolutes. The standards are there and our job is to try to fulfil them. Because we are less than perfect and live in a world which is very far from being perfect, there will be conflict over these standards, and deep and genuine problems as we try to apply them to the moving circumstances and changing issues that face us. This is a summons to even harder work, not an escape from difficulty. Nor is it an excuse for escaping from the real world. Rather it is an invitation to get stuck into that world. That we end up in conflict situations, where one standard has to be set above or below another standard, does not mean that we have no standards, or that they are unimportant. On the contrary, it is our very commitment to them that requires us to be faithful to them in realistically applying them to the issues today.

Insights and application

Christians believe that God is the maker of heaven and earth, and creator of all humanity. In making men and women in his image, in endowing us all with consciences, and in so structuring the world that there are basic natural guidelines for human being and flourishing, God has revealed his will in a general way to us all. It is, and ought to be, no surprise to find moral insights wherever humanity lives and functions. Human goodness is to be found as part of being created, and moral insight can be learned from many different sources and settings. The Christian seeks to gain such insight in the light of God's revelation in Christ and in Scripture, and to apply it to the realities of human existence.

As we have seen, God's gift of the Spirit enables us to apply God's standards to particular cases and settings, and to do what God demands of us and commands us to do.

Whole people

The Bible teaches that men and women are complex beings. We dare not reduce them to one level or facet. This holds good in moral decision-making. Of course, our feelings are involved, and so they should be. We prefer to have those who care deeply to look after us and to make decisions which affect us directly, rather than those who feel nothing and care in no way whatsoever. In similar ways, our wills do matter. We can will and choose, and we can fail to do so. What we choose, and how much we commit ourselves to those choices, makes a great deal of difference to all of us. But to isolate the will and the emotions from each other and from our thinking and reasoning is a nonsense. We are whole people, and our morality should express the importance of every aspect of our being in the moral choices and decisions we have to make. So, for the Christian, to omit all reference to God, and to our responsibility to him to use our thinking, feeling and willing, fails to do justice to the whole person. Our moral decision-making must seek wholeness for all because we are made in the image of God.

The Christian community

Christianity demands that each and every individual should recognize for himself or herself that we ought to live in harmony with God and his will for our lives. But that never means doing it all alone. Likewise, when we face up to the complexity of applying the absolute standards to our different situations and contexts, we do not do this alone. It is as part of the Christian community that we function.

This Christian community is a community of millions down through history. We are part of a great tradition of men and women who have tried to be faithful to the heavenly vision. We have much to learn from their example and teaching. There are examples to be copied and other lessons to be avoided. We are who we are largely as a result of the tradition of the church and those who have gone before us in the life of faith.

But it is equally true that we are members of and with each other in the Christian life here and now. As part of the living organism of the church, we find a setting and the support we need as we discuss and debate the moral issues that face twentieth-century men and women and thus discern the mind of Christ. The Bible could not hope to cover every question that faced people when it was written. Even less can we expect to find direct answers to the new moral dilemmas that science and technology create. Yet we have in the community of God's people a group and a setting where we can try to understand the implications of God's Word for life today. Morality is far too important to be left to us philosophers in our ivory towers. It is the whole church, in the light of Scripture and tradition, which seeks to know the mind of Christ by the direction of his Holy Spirit.

So what?

This book argues that we can find right and wrong only in terms of God. No other view is fully adequate, though each may offer crucial insights and lessons from which we can learn. But it would be a strange book about right and wrong that concluded by suggesting that any one *theory* is better than any other. The only real test for morality is in living it. So the challenge with which I want to conclude this book is that we begin to be like Jesus or continue to grow more like him. Only then shall we know whether Christian morality is really right or wrong in every sense.